MUZAK®

THE HIDDEN MESSAGES IN MUSIC

MUZAK®

THE HIDDEN MESSAGES IN MUSIC

A Social Psychology of Culture

STEPHEN H. BARNES

Studies on The History and Interpretation of Music
Volume 9

The Edwin Mellen Press
Lewiston/Queenston

Library of Congress Cataloging-in-Publication Data

Barnes, Stephen H.
Muzak, the hidden messages in music : a social psychology of culture / Stephen H. Barnes.
p. cm. -- (Studies in the history and interpretation of music ; v. 9)
Includes index.
ISBN 0-88946-434-0
1. Muzak (Registered trademark) 2. Music, Influence of. 3. Music--Psychology. 4. Music in industry. I. Title. II. Series.
ML3920.B23 1988
781'.15--dc19

87-31951
CIP
MN

This is volume 9 in the continuing series
Studies In History & Interpretation Of Music
ISBN 0-88946-434-0
SHIM Series 0-88946-426-X

The Edwin Mellen Press
Box 450
Lewiston, New York
USA 14092

The Edwin Mellen Press
Box 67
Queenston, Ontario
L0S 1L0 CANADA

Printed in the United States of America

CONTENTS

LIST OF TABLES

LIST OF FIGURES

LIST OF ILLUSTRATIONS

In Memory of

Randall Acton Barnes

PART I

THE MUSIC YOU LOVE TO HATE

Muzak promotes the sharing of meaning because it massifies symbolism in which not few but all can participate.

James Keenan, Ph. D.
Chairman, Board of
Scientific Advisors
Muzak Corporation

Chapter 1

GENERAL SQUIER'S INVENTION

"I have Muzak in every room of my home. Twenty-four hours a day. We sleep with it on, watch TV with it on. I never allow it to be turned off because I know that music has a therapeutic, psychological value."

Muzak Franchise Holder

1986. Those with a broad historical perspective had many things to commemorate that year, such as the sesquicentennial of Texas, the 350th anniversary of the founding of Harvard College, the 350th anniversary of the first Sunday school in Savannah, the 200th anniversary of Miss Liberty in New York Harbor, and the 50th anniversary of Muzak's first commercial operations. Muzak? Shouldn't 1936 be remembered for something else? Like Jesse Owens' performance in the Olympic Games, the development of the Vice President's flag or the invention of the first glass, screw-cap bottle with a lip for pouring?

The sound of Muzak *is* everywhere -- in the bank, supermarket, office elevator, and even on the telephone when the poor victim has been put on hold. It played at the 1984 Olympics and on the Apollo XI spacecraft that took Neil Armstrong and Buzz Aldrin to the moon. It plays at the White House and at the Pentagon. One hundred million people everyday, in twenty-five countries, are subjected to it. Muzak is big business. Now a part of Westinghouse's Group W operations, the company and its affiliates take in over $150 million annually.

Muzak's soothing the top brass daily in the Pentagon is only fitting. The original concept was essentially the creation of an unusual general, George O. Squier. Squier was a West Point graduate (Class of 1887) and a decorated World War I veteran. He devoted much of his military career to science, flying a Wright biplane in 1908 on orders from the Army, evaluating the military potential of the new invention and, as a young artillery officer, inventing the polarizing photochronograph to measure the speed of a projectile. Upon entry of the United States into the Great War, Squier became chief of the Signal Corps. His keen curiosity led to a notable invention, a system for transmitting several messages *simultaneously* over existing electric power lines.

In 1922, General Squier, nearing retirement, took his patents to the North American Company, a public utilities holding company that had once financed Thomas Edison. That relationship had led to the creation of General Electric. The North American company bought Squier's plan launching Wired Radio, Incorporated. Wired Radio was to compete with the booming fad for wireless radio by using electric power lines to transmit news programs, music, lectures, general entertainment and advertising directly into private homes. It was not until 1934, the year of General Squier's death, however, that he developed a catchy new name for his product combining "music" with the trade name of the most popular camera of the time, Kodak, hence, Muzak.

Muzak was clearly a novelty, and would have become as obsolete as the stereopticon of an earlier era had it not been for some experiments in the 1930's showing that music could get more work out of people. One early study conducted at the Stevens Institute of Technology in New Jersey demonstrated that this new "functional music" reduced absenteeism in the workplace by 88 percent and early departures by 53 percent. Other experiments produced even more interesting findings. When Muzak was piped into a McKeesport, Pennsylvania farm, the cows gave more milk; the music inspired chickens to lay more eggs.

In a far more serious vein, the coming of World War II made the novelty more than a matter of money: literally thousands of U. S. factories, shipyards, and arsenals were wired for Muzak, and production increased by as high as 11 percent.

Muzak does not rest on its laurels; it is still conducting its studies. At a firm in Charlottesville, Virginia called Precision Small Parts, Inc., for example, Muzak spent three months in 1983 testing six women who spent their work days drearily deburring very small objects with dental drills. They deburred 16.8 percent more with Muzak oozing into their ears. Other tests showed that sedately paced melodies in a supermarket *slowed* down customers so that they spent 38 percent more money.

"Environmental music" *does* work particularly for people subject to either stress or boredom. Functional music is soothing. Moreover, Muzak even claims that its recordings make workers feel more in control of the environment and more cared for by their employers. The irony should not be lost here. It is, of course, the workers who are being controlled and manipulated by their employers. Yes, manipulated. As workers slow down in mid-morning and mid-afternoon, music programmed by Muzak counteracts this fatigue. This is the concept of stimulus progression. Each tune is given a stimulus code based on its tempo, instrumentation, feel, and date it was added to the corporation's library. The codes are punched into Muzak's computer which slots the material into fifteen-minute segments of five tunes each. The set starts with a piece that is slow in tempo and string instrument dominated. Succeeding pieces gradually build up the tempo, instrumentation and intensity. After a pause, a new segment begins on a stimulus level that's higher than the ones preceding. In this manner, the day's program builds to mid-morning and mid-afternoon peak points designed to give workers a needed lift. Muzak notes that "around ten-thirty, you're running down a little, but lunch is still a distance away. So, at about ten-fifteen, the stimulus value for the entire segment jumps an extra notch to bring you out of the doldrums."

Muzak's affect is no trivial matter. Changing the order of the pieces produces a different result, a stimulus regression, if you will. The corporation claims that when the so-called ascending program is played in reverse, it seems to lull people to sleep. Reaction times are reported to be slower and more variable.

Muzak darts into the ear, does its subtle job in the subcortex of the brain, then slips out the other ear without saying hello or goodbye. The listener is all but unaware that anything has been perceived, but the music has sloshed around inside his head, and, relieved of the humdrum exercise of thinking, the listener feels better. The only thing to fear is extended silence. To win such willing ears, Muzak keeps things very simple and undemanding -- guided always by its sole aesthetic tenet: the music must be unobtrusive. There is no jazz, vocal, or classical music. Instrumental solos, pieces in the minor mode (too sad) and *anything* more than three minutes in length is also *verboten.* Ensuring that Muzak never intrudes are a program director, ten musicologists and thirty-five arrangers who all strive for the *functional* sound. Muzak does all its own recordings, turning the raw product over to the engineers who squeeze the dynamic range to a maximum of twenty-five decibels (compared to fifty on a normal LP). Before being added to Muzak's 7,000-piece library, the arrangement is screened by the musicologists and arrangers. Anything in the music that grasps their attention is cause for immediate surgery. The offending element is neatly cut out by the magic of modern electronics. Once in a while, an arrangement may get into their library which is far too stimulating or distracting for Muzak's purposes. The mistake is realized when, for instance, subscribers or their employees request a certain number or simply express their liking of an arrangement. Muzak responds immediately by taking the arrangement out of the library to be reworked.

Once added to the tape library, the specially created piece is strategically protected. Muzak plays its melodies from inside locked chambers. Once per day, the Muzak person enters to reprogram the tapes. It is certainly a comfort to know that the machines are linked in such a manner that even as Armageddon is fought, Muzak will continue to play untended.

Yes, simple and undemanding; and consider the sameness of it all. Muzak has just three standard programs -- Office, Factory, and Public Area Muzak. The Office and Factory programs are delivered to the customers on alternate quarter hours around the clock. Public Area Muzak, a combination of the two, plays constantly. Diners have their appetites involuntarily triggered by the same musical arrangements that increase the efficiency of riveters. Women listening to Muzak via earphones in beauty salon hair dryers are comforted in knowing that their spouses are hearing the same piece over at the waste treatment plant. By pursuing unobtrusiveness musically and programmatically, Muzak achieves its goal. It produces music to be utterly ignored. Or, viewed with the paradoxical clarity of Zen: boring work is made less boring by boring music. For all the emphasis by Muzak on remedying the workers' situations in offices and factories, the victims working in commercial establishments are virtually forgotten. The Public Area Muzak is intended, of course, for a *transient* audience. However, the employees cannot escape this constant musical background. The waiters, cashiers, and hat check girls, getting a steady dose of Public Area Muzak are understandably irritable and are probably in need of a counter-Muzak service.

Muzak is nevertheless a universal language. Women workers in a flour mill in Argentina used to fight and shout at each other on sight. Enter Muzak. Now they go to work peaceably to a soft, musical accompaniment. The "light industrial program" offered by the Muzak people has, for over twenty years, been piped into a Stuttgart brothel.

Bland it may be, but Muzak also inflames people. A worker at Ford's Dearborn plant says, "It's so faint, it sounds like angels singing -- and that's hell to work with." Muzak counters by pointing out that "the nut who bitches about music is the same one who bitches about the office being too cold or too hot. We feel that anyone who doesn't like music doesn't believe in God." Quite a paradox. Muzak says its polls show repeatedly that more than 85 percent of its customers enjoy what they get from the company which now broadcasts the tunes by satellite from Stamford, Connecticut to 180 receiving stations around the country.

Why hate it so passionately? Some believe that this system perverts and prostitutes one of the great pleasures of life: *listening* to music. With any other medium, one can turn away or close one's eyes, but there really is no escape from music. An executive whose company uses Muzak in all its plants was once quoted as saying, "It's like wallpaper. If it's not there, you miss it; but it makes you feel good without distracting you from your work." It apparently mattered not in the least to him that Muzak is one of the major influences in our time which is gradually planting in the minds of millions of people the idea that music is something to be subliminally heard but never listened to -- a comforting noise perpetually in the background of our lives.

Muzak then can hardly be taken lightly. To be sure, the programmed environmental or functional music produced by companies such as the Muzak Corporation has been the butt of many jokes. But don't take it lightly. Humor is most effective when dealing with those areas of life wherein we are at once deeply concerned and yet uncertain. It's no accident that so much of our humor concerns sex, religion, and politics. Try to turn this initial laughter into a *serious* discussion of functional music, in this instance, and some very impassioned opinions will come to the surface.

Too often, these opinions betray a virtual ignorance of the subject. Most of us simply try to ignore functional music, if we can. If we happen to *listen* to it, our musical tastes are invariably insulted and, with or without comment, we usually just leave it at that. After all, such a tastelass form of music seems unworthy of further consideration. This is a mistake. Functional music needs to be understood if only because of its astounding pervasiveness. Only seven of the 150 largest corporations in the United States are *not* Muzak clients.

And Muzak is not the only company involved in functional

music. The 3M Corporation, for example, accounts for approximately twenty-five percent of the business, and there are a number of other firms involved to lesser extent, such as Tape-Athon, Inc., the Ditchburn Organization, Rowe International, and Magnetronics, Inc. No figures are available on the exact number of people exposed to functional music daily, but the figure would certainly give one pause. Certainly functional music accounts for a majority of the music heard, figured by listening hours *per capita*, in the U.S. We may dislike it, but on a number of levels, it's damn difficult to ignore. So some make fun of it. For instance, there's the story of the woman wih a Viennese accent who was chattering blithely about her shopping exploits when she and her male companion entered an already crowded elevator in the lobby of a large New York hotel. Put off by the glumness of the less-than-convivial humanity packed around her, she fell into silence as the elevator car began its ascent to the Starlite Lounge. Suddenly, two Muzak speakers concealed in the elevator's ceiling commenced a bland rendition of an Irving Berlin ballad. Astonished and smiling, the lady from Vienna smiled, looked upward, and exclaimed to her escort: "How charming! This hotel has music sprinklers!"

Certainly Muzak has created, with this woman as an example, the quintessential captive audience. An individual is literally trapped in the elevator and, as he or she watches the doors slide shut, is subjected to an emasculated version of something like the *Surrey with the Fringe on Top*. Some individuals neither try to ignore Muzak nor make jokes about it. Some take it head on. The most noted instance was a run-in with John Cage, the avant-garde composer.

Cage, born in Los Angeles in 1912, is a classically-trained composer famous (or *infamous*) for such compositions as *Music for Amplified Toy Pianos* (1960) and 0'00", an indempotent "to be performed in any way by anyone"(1962).* Cage and Muzak

*Cage's most notorious work is *4 Minutes and 33 Seconds* which requires a piano soloist to sit in silence for four minutes and thirty-three seconds staring at a stopwatch before departing the stage without playing a note.

tangled in the early 1960's when the composer was presented with a difficult problem involving Manhattan's Pan American Building. Richard Lippold, a sculptor noted for his shiny geometric constructions of stainless steel and gold, had been commissioned by the directors of the Pan Am Building to design a piece for the main lobby. Lippold crafted *The Globe*, a huge, glittering work standing three stories high. The directors were delighted, Sculptor Lippold was not. He learned that Muzak would be piped into the lobby and the building's elevators, its ooze an unwanted invasion destroying the impact of his bold design. Crying "foul," he called on Cage for assistance with the Pan Am directors' blessing.

Cage's suggestion for the music was as daring as the sculpture. He decided to make use of the objects at hand, i.e., the Muzak speakers and the closed-circuit television cameras set up to monitor the lobby -- both systems being already in place. Cage wanted the TV to trigger Muzak whenever people passed by or entered or exited the elevators. But instead of the usual *Londonderry Air* or *Stardust*, Cage offered to re-pulverize and filter the music electronically. He also recommended that since there might be occasions when foot traffic was light, there would be times when his arrangements would not be played at all! Just silence. The Pan Am directors vetoed the ideas. An official representing Pan Am noted, "The American businessman and the esthete do not always see eye to eye."

The bottom line? No music at all in the Pan Am lobby. Cage and Lippold were not interested in corrupting their art with the modern-day version of General Squier's invention.

Chapter 2

THE SCIENCE OF ERGONOMICS

That very afternoon I began shaking hands with Muzak men. Almost all were youngish (under forty-five); all were business card carriers. In the ensuing week I never had to ask a man how he spelled his name without receiving a business card, and with each card came the verbal admonition: "Don't print my name."

Adapted from Alan Levy
in "The Muzak Men" in
Horizon. September, 1962

Ergonomics is defined by the *International Labour Review* as "using *engineered* methods to humanize work areas." Ergonomy measures the effect of air-conditioning, lighting and furniture on productivity and includes music, a powerful manipulative tool. Musical ergonomics have their genesis as far back as Ivan Petrovich Pavlov's experiments on the conditioned reflex. In order to stay ahead of its competition, Muzak has encouraged ergonomics research. It has commissioned it, sponsored it, verified it, and exploited it. In fact, it was Muzak's own engineering breakthroughs in the 1950's that perfected magnetic tape transmission and led not only to near total automation, but also to the corporation's most significant spurt in growth. (It was in the interval between 1953 and 1957 that the number of Muzak franchisers nearly doubled to 154. Today, in 1988, there are approximately two hundred.) A Muzak official once told a Pittsburgh audience that a properly planned program of work music can "give workers a sense of privacy by masking conversation and other noises while unifying an office staff by giving individual employees something in common."

Muzak seldom sells its product to labor. Pitches for installation are made at the presidential level or just slightly below. The *company* has to decide it wants Muzak. Management sometimes gives it as a gift to labor. Sometimes workers request it of the company, but Muzak has found that, when they do, they rarely get it.

Muzak's corporate pitch is frighteningly straightforward. "We're not selling background music. We're selling the ability to motivate people in work situations. The vechicle is Muzak. It's music with a purpose. Muzak points out that a "tense, emotional" labor force costs industry three billion dollars a year. Muzak eases tension as surely as aspirin eases a headache. Prospective buyers of Muzak's services listen to an "Anti-Competitive Tape," the weapon used to demonstrate to prospective clients why Muzak leads its rivals. The tape begins with the news that "of the twenty-five largest American companies, over eighty percent are Muzak subscribers." These companies rely on Muzak because "it's scientifically applied to improve worker morale." As the narrator speaks, the Muzak tinkles.

Suddenly, narrator and Muzak stop. The silence is deafening. When the narrator's voice returns momentarily, it is as reassuring as an all-clear siren: "Without Muzak, noise and even silence become noticeable, distracting." (The impossibility of a working life *without* Muzak, once a company is hooked, plays a role in the nearly 100 percent renewal rate when subscribers' three-to-five year commitment expires.)

The "Anti-Competitive Tape" proceeds to a lush romantic arrangement of a popular tune. The narrator comes on and says "Dreamy, wasn't it? But of course there's no place for dreaming in work situations." The same popular tune immediately reappears -- this time in a jazz arrangement. "Can you imagine *this* being played in *your* office?" the pitchman asks. Before one can indicate "no," the tune reappears in a third arrangement: the Muzak version. It is as invigorating as a menthol cigarette and planned to get the prospective subscriber's signature on the bottom line.

Ergonomics is a new science and, as noted earlier, even Muzak sometimes goofs. Contracted to begin programming for the Buenos Aires area, Muzak in the 1950's sent tapes containing only Latin-American tunes. They found that the sambas and tangos were just as attention-grabbing south of the border as they would be here. Muzak switched to the same tapes that people receive in the United States. Lesson learned: since their music is all-functional it makes no difference, people *respond* to Muzak the same way everywhere. Well, almost. Although Muzak uses no lyrics or vocalists, its audiences often know the words.

Some years ago, a plane taxiing toward its assigned runway had to return to the terminal when Muzak offered *For All We Know* and a woman passenger became hysterical. Those lyrics begin "For All We Know/We may never meet again . . ." (Muzak otherwise carefully censors its travel package which rides trains, planes, ships, and buses in a shoe-box size device monitored by porters, drivers and/or flight attendants.) Banned on airline flights are, *I've Got a Feeling I'm Falling, The High and the Mighty, With a Little Bit of Luck,* and *Stormy Weather.* A Florida-based flight might sneak in *Moon Over Miami* and a Honolulu-based flight, *Yankee Hula Hickey Doola.* Hawaiian music, however, is taboo on Muzak's industrial or office programs. It tends to set a slow work pace and promote escapism. You'll never hear *Deep in the Heart of Texas* on Muzak or songs that might inspire clapping, hymns, or distracting fanfares.

Franchisers are permitted little programming leeway. For special occasions such as St. Patrick's Day or Christmas, franchisers can inject Irish jigs or carols from special equipment. Officially, however, the guidelines are strict. Muzak recommends the injection of one Christmas song per hour starting December 1, two starting December 5, three starting December 12, and four beginning on December 19.

Muzak zealously guards against piracy and tampering. Each tape is carefully routed to its franchises, and upon return to the home office, is monitored before erased. Each tape is inaudibly and indelibly impressed with the Muzak trademark. If played on any non-Muzak equipment, the tape chirps M-U-Z-A-K in Morse code, in signal-corps fashion, for all to hear.

Muzak claims that it receives negative reactions from no more than three to five percent of the population: elderly spinsters, just-contrary-people, individualists, and people who think that, because they know something about music, they know about Muzak. Opponents of its bland product make more noise than their numbers would indicate, claims Muzak, and the corporation refers to them as the "vocal minority."

In reality, most of the negative comments about Muzak's functional product come from employees in commercial establishments. These individuals receive a constant dose of the Public Area Muzak while working in restaurants, shopping malls, supermarkets and department stores, these establishments comprising thirty percent of Muzak's subscribers. Here the sophisticated stimulus progression technique serves no purpose at all, of course. Obviously, Muzak cannot "serve" both transient customers and employees in the same manner. The solution to the dilemma was natural enough: direct the music at the customers, who, after all, are bringing profits to the store. Thus the employee gets subjected to continuous music, even though industrial psychologists have known for some time that such endless sound is useless in combating fatigue or boredom. Thus, whatever manipulative power the music has in these situations, it affects only customers. As in the industrial or business environment, the music masks unpleasant realities in the external environment (the noise of shopping carts, cash registers, clattering silverware, voices) or within our own minds (negative thoughts, moods, the price of what you're buying, etc.).

Masking extraneous sounds is one thing, masking silence is another. For whatever reasons, our society is deathly afraid of silence, even though one rarely experiences true silence even in its approximately pure form. Muzak is well aware of this morbid fear of silence, noting in a list of Muzak's "proven benefits" its ability to "fill in the deadly silences."

Functional music then can be added to the elements making up the science of ergonomics. It is another of the factors used to influence us subconsciously and joins the variables of architectural design, the use of colors, lighting, heating, and air-conditioning. However, we can be manipulated only insofar as we remain unconscious of these influences.

Chapter 3

CALLING THE TUNE

We don't want to astound or horrify people.

Rod Baum, Vice President for Programming, Muzak Corporation

Muzak goes beyond a prostitution of one of life's great pleasures, i.e., *listening* to music; Muzak manipulates. Muzak and similar functional musics should not be regarded as a benign fixture of the workplace or eating establishment. Otherwise, why would retailers, employers, industrialists, and entrepreneurs spend millions of dollars annually on Muzak? The answer, of course, is subtle manipulation. Workers, customers, and clients are being "had" by the human engineers at Muzak. Why is there no public outcry about this? Certainly any other form of mass manipulation of this type would be so vilified and rejected that it would easily qualify in most minds as unscrupulous, illegal, and certainly *un-American.* Parents of teenagers urge Congress and the record industry to begin rating phonograph records as G, PG13, R, X and the like, fearful that playing these discs (either forward or *backward*) might lead to anti-social behavior. How ironic. These parents instinctively know that there is *power* in music. They've got *that* part correct. But it is the parents who are being manipulated by a subliminal stimulus produced by a corporation which has had one line officer bearing the title, Director of Human Engineering. Granted, there is no threat here of developing anti-social behavior; the manipulation is in the other direction. Muzak is a palliative. Muzak relieves tension and stress without removing the causes of the tension and stress. It lets us adjust to our environment instead of really changing it. Their promotional material says, "Muzak programs are designed to combat tension, fatigue and stress which are ever-increasing by-products of our environment . . ." Considering the domestic and international scope of its operation in twenty-five countries affecting one hundred million workers, shoppers, and travelers daily, Muzak easily qualifies as the greatest single example of world-wide pacification in recorded history.

William Wokoun once carried the title of Director of Human Engineering for the Muzak Corporation. A trained psychologist with a doctorate from the University of Nebraska, Wokoun's first postdoctoral job was with the U.S. Army Human Engineering Laboratories in Maryland as a research psychologist, and, subsequently, the writer of a course on human engineering for Army personnel. He was also a lecturer on motivation at the Edgewood Arsenal in Maryland. (This continuing link between the Army and Muzak one might find curious.) Wokoun found his military training useful in his position with Muzak. A study in the late 60's on the effect of programmed music on vigilance, which was conducted by the Army at the Human Engineering Laboratories, Aberdeen Proving Grounds, not only employed arrangements from the Muzak library, but was actually a government-sponsored experiment to determine if the Muzak approach does, indeed, work. It did. The researchers determined that a planned program of music prepared by Muzak, based on the principles the corporation had been using for some time, improved the vigilance of soldiers manning sophisticated missile systems.

Vigilance for the Army, pacification for the retailer. If the store manager chooses to save money by stationing only one check-out clerk when several are required to handle the traffic, the manager uses functional music to keep the customers quiet while they wait in long lines. Consider this testimonial, "The music tends to have a soothing effect on the customers. They aren't as edgy while waiting in line . . ." If that weren't enough, programmed music ". . . can also distract attention from the total cost of a shopping cart full of merchandise." The soothing effects of functional music are even used to pacify harried investors. Walston and Company, an investment firm, noted that "when the market is volatile, Muzak has a soothing effect." The intent of background music-makers is hardly covert when the promotional materials announce that "managers . . . are discovering that people, along with machines, need to be programmed."

Study after study shows that Muzak is an effective management tool. The studies are impressive and frightening, and there is no quarrel with the methodology: the research reports provided by the Muzak Corporation show studies reasonably well-done and employing appropriate methodology. One study, conducted by Case and Company, a management consultant firm, investigated the effects Muzak had on productivity and other factors at the American Machine and Foundry Company in Brooklyn, New York. These workers were *not* the usual assembly-line types; they were highly skilled assemblers engaged in non-repetitive activity requiring individual judgment. Muzak was installed in one department while a second, comparable department served as the experimental control. (Any changes in personnel and production in the Muzak department would be attributed to Muzak.) The study ran for months. With Muzak, efficiency in the department rose 2.8 percent, while the efficiency in the entire plant likewise declined at a 3.6 percent rate. Muzak works. In addition, despite the fact that the weather conditions during the study would normally have resulted in an increase in worker tardiness, the reverse was true. Muzak had a positive effect curbing employee lateness.

Another study, independently conducted by the management engineering firm of Stevenson, Jordan and Harrison, Inc., was carefully designed to obtain accurate data and to avoid extraneous factors including the Hawthorne Effect: workers increasing their productivity because they are receiving more attention than normal, in effect, "pleasing" the experimenter. The results were again impressive. At Lever Brothers, the productivity of a typing pool rose steadily during the time

Muzak was played and declined steadily after its removal. The functional music was credited with a 36.8 percent decrease in typing errors.

So what. Doesn't management have the right to use Muzak to increase productivity? Well, it depends on your value system. This manipulation can be costly in terms of human welfare; the Muzak Corporation even admits it. In one of their promotional pamphlets, Muzak quotes M.S. Viteles, an industrial psychologist:

> In nearly all occupations an increasing strain and intensity of labor are stimulated by modern methods of production. A survey of changes of methods of work has led to the opinion that although machinery, in a sense, has lightened the burden of toil, it has not reduced fatigue in the worker . . . The introduction of machinery and the specialization of labor have made it possible to increase greatly the speed of individual workers . . . price rate(s) and other financial incentives . . . further urge on the worker to a faster pace. The increased tension under such conditions of work appears to offset the savings in muscular force made possible by the machine. The tension, the speed, the subjection to specialization of work and rhythm uncontrolled by the individual promote *fatigue*, characterized by a decrease in the power to work.

Functional music counteracts fatigue, which is the lack of *power* to work *not* the lack of desire or will to work. It manipulates the workers' minds, masking their perception of their own physical state. Through stimulus progression, Muzak counteracts the *normal*, daily onset of fatigue. It is ironic to note that the history of American trade unionism has been inextricably bound to the fight against the most dehumanizing aspects of the workplace including speed-ups. How interesting then to have a speed-up tool that is liked by the workers involved. Muzak supplies its customers with an elaborate apology for this manipulation which appears to contradict the material they quote from M.S. Viteles. Most psychologists, a Muzak promotional folder states:

> agree that about ninety-five percent of fatigue in people who are physically well is psychological, a fact which many people find difficult to accept. But, in fact, *fatigue is often a defense mechanism.* Boredom is associated with fatigue. The repetition of the same, somewhat mechanical duties . . . can be fatiguing and boring. (Italics mine)

Notice how the definition of fatigue has been modified from "a decrease in the power to work" to "boredom." Certainly boredom and alienation play a part in causing fatigue, but to attribute ninety-five percent of fatigue to psychological factors would appear to encourage the worst kind of sweatshop slave driving.

What then is the role of boredom and alienation and how do these psychological factors contribute to the cause of fatigue? Certainly boredom and alienation contribute to fatigue and we know that, overall, defense mechanisms spring from the very human and genuine need to protect one's own physical and emotional health. So if fatigue is sometimes a defense mechanism, what then is the root cause? What is causing people to be defensive? Muzak doesn't answer these questions that deal with these fundamental, underlying principles. It is easier to treat the symptoms.

The Muzak Corporation recognizes that alienation exists. One bit of their material states that "since the Industrial Revolution with its increasing emphasis on technological and productive advances, the worker has become increasingly alienated from his job." Muzak, of course, bridges the ". . . widening gap between his desires and his needs." It appears then that Muzak has decided what workers need. Most of today's work is boring; employees have little control over the quality and conditions of their work situations and little knowledge or insight of the production process overall and how their role fits into it. These have a physiological effect, i.e., producing fatigue, which is of minimal concern to the management analyst, but the fact that fatigue decreased worker productivity *is.* Functional music in the workplace is designed to improve worker morale, to distract the employee from his or her alienated condition and feelings of powerlessness, to act as a palliative, and to boost productivity, but not to alter the basic conditions that are the root cause of the boredom and alienation in the first place.

Muzak plays with your body as well as your mind. The effects of music, including Muzak, are not just psychological. Although Muzak claims to be interested primarily in the psychological effects of music, their brochures quite correctly quote studies which show that music increases bodily metabolism, changes mental energy, accelerates respiration and decreases its regularity, and produces a definite but variable effect (differing from one individual to the next) on pulse rate and blood pressure. Music has a definite effect on galvanic skin response. Actually it would be hard to prove that functional music has become so sophisticated as to "program" employees' pulse rates and levels of muscular energy. As mentioned, the reactions vary from individual to individual. Even Muzak indicates that "there is little except generalities in public print" on these physiological effects of music. It's a fascinating and frightening prospect, however.

Functional music thus consists of the application of the physiological and psychological effects of music to produce a *predetermined* result. In this instance, it is the ultimate perversion of this art form. Music represents merely the *raw material* or a means to an end and not the end in itself. It doesn't matter whether the music is good or not or if critically-thinking people like it, as long as it works.

Individuals who criticize functional music most strongly are exactly those persons for whom it is *not* intended. This group includes musicians and music lovers; with them the music often causes boredom, restlessness, or simple irritation. Studying individual reactions to functional music is not, however, as simple as it might seem. Most people hear it only on a subconscious level. A common response to pollsters checking on Muzak's acceptance is "what music?" or "I don't listen to it." These individuals are, of course *hearing* the music but not *listening* to it. Another typical response runs like this: "No, I never listen to it. But now that you ask, I really don't like it." The respondents are, of course, being asked to evaluate something which is designed to affect only their subconscious minds. This *conscious* evaluation does have significance, though, even if it doesn't say much about one's normal, non-evaluating state in relation to Muzak. If enough people decide *consciously* that they resent functional music, it might not be as pervasive in our society as it is. However, it is pervasive in our modern industrial society for the simple reason that it produces concrete results measurable in dollars and cents.

Muzak constantly tries to emphasize its humane, benevolent, and scientific nature. "We research, test, evaluate, develop and arrange good music for good human goals" and "Muzak helps human communities because it is a nonverbal symbolism for the common stuff of everyday living in the global village." And for the beleaguered capitalist, Muzak is a means for fighting "the constant struggle to improve productivity or cut production costs." In the workplace, of course, the real enemy is not so much Muzak as it is the workplace itself. Our modern industrial society is often noisy, generally boring, and typically vulgar. Muzak's continual success depends on these adverse conditions in the workplace. They know that there is alienation and boredom. They know that four out of five young, blue collar workers are bored with their jobs. White collar boredom is only slightly less significant. Muzak promises to remedy this by making the "work seem easier and faster."

Muzak, seen in this light, appears to be a temporary restraining measure in a long, unresolved conflict. And, of course, it is. Muzak may make the work *seem* easier, but the work is really no less repetitive or unfulfilling. The symptoms

-- tedium, monotony, boredom, labor-management friction are treated; the causes -- miniscule divisions of labor and worker-management role conflict, are accepted as givens. Without a modification of our value system, we can expect no less than this "Muzak Society" to continue and flourish. This "Muzak Society" is characterized by an alarming passivity that has been created and sustained by a number of interacting influences -- historical, economic and legal. These influences, the origins of the Muzak Society, are explored next.

PART II

THE ORIGINS OF THE MUZAK SOCIETY

The sound that says, "Everything is going to be all right."

Muzak, 1981

Chapter 4

THE FINE SCIENCE OF MANAGING LABOR

"Our whole job in life is to increase production and lower errors in any work situation."

Muzak Spokesman

The origins of the Muzak Society can be found in the Industrial Revolution which began in England in the 17th and 18th centuries and which arrived subsequently in the United States in the 19th and 20th centuries. The changes brought about were more than mere advances in technology; for workers, centuries of pre industrial living had established set social patterns, rhythms, and perceptions of time. The rise of industry and the development of the factory system would prove to be a formidable challenge to the old order and result in a transformation of unparalleled proportions.

This enormous transformation was characterized by an emerging conformity by the workers to the conditions of the new workplace, the factory. Accompanying this transformation, i.e., the development of a modern industrial labor force were two types of social dislocation: (1) a virulent growth in terms of urbanization and (2) a cross cultural tension resulting from the immigration of peoples from non industrial countries. Each ethnic group coped in its own fashion with the dehumanizing aspects of factory life and attempted to resist the nonhuman, mechanical rhythms of the new industrial rationality. To this day, that process continues. Put another way, industrialization, as a process, is more than producing more goods in a new fashion. It involves a new conception of socialization which attempts to legitimately stabilize and control those persons whose work is required for the production of goods.

The question of social control is a recurring issue in the history of industrial capitalism. Early on, i.e., the start of the

19th century, the issue of social stability and control was related to the question of labor. The new, industrial workplace required a constant pool of laborers whose productivity could be predicted and be made more statistically reliable. The inevitable conflict that developed between the industrialist's requirement for a dependable labor force and the pre industrial, agrarian populace led to a significant amount of physical and psychological tension and, later, violence. In short, the traditional, normal work ethic of these individuals contrasted sharply with the requirements of the factory.

It is the critical concept of *time* that most accurately brings the industrial and non industrial production modes into contrast. The mechanical time clock of the factory is an incredibly effective agent of negative discipline; it's an assault upon the temporal sense of a people who had heretofore maintained a concept of *timeliness* based on the periodicities of the sun, moon, stars, and seasons. Time was simply measured in large units based upon an agricultural way of life. In introducing people to the factory work process, a whole new time concept had to be internalized -- one built on the rhythms of mechanical prodution and the industrial workday. Looking at it from a different angle, the mechanical method of goods-production could not be established and thrive without the workers accepting the social psychological processes required to support them. The workers had to internalize a new, industrialized society by transforming their sense of time and all that this distinct sense assists in the organizing and defining of activity.

Resistance to the growth of industrial capitalism by the workers was widespread in the early 20th century. It was apparent that if the industrial system were to survive, an accommodation had to occur. That accommodation rested on the development of an industrial system that would meet the people's needs: the bond linking work and misery in the minds and activities of the workers had to be broken. The industrialists resisted at first; there were violent attacks on organized labor.

The stability of the industrial system was in question and it is no wonder that the capitalists were aided legally by the use of the military, state and local police. The open resistance was quieted. Yet a smoldering militancy remained, and, recognizing this deep feeling, it was evident that what was needed was a *new* social instrumentality which could defuse and neutralize worker-dissatisfaction and unrest. It was a social imperative and a matter of survival. This instrumentality, hailed as further evidence of the industrial evolution, came to be called *labor management.* Thus the industrialists coped with the twin devils of labor unrest and civil strife in the same fashion that they dealt with the inanimate, material resource problems of industrial production. They formed a *systematic*, i.e., "scientific" approach to the problem.

Heretofore, labor management had been an issue only when the labor force was scarce. Entrepreneurial concern, in the earliest days of industrialization, was certainly not addressed to labor management, i.e., the utilization of a means to develop, organize, and control any given workforce. Pressures of the marketplace and the proper use of coercion combined to control the labor force. In actuality, two internal forces kept things in line: workers were managed by a value-system which extolled craftsmanship and by the more legalized system of the master-servant relationship, or, at least, the master-apprentice ethic. Obviously, such an inefficient pattern was not acceptable in the new industrial society. The nature of the clash between the traditional work ethic and the demands of the new order is striking and compelling. Traditional skilled labor was accomplished at either a leisurely pace or in a spurt of intensity at the *discretion* of the worker. Such variances are unacceptable in modern industry: work must be done at a uniform intensity. In a traditional setting, the skilled laborer worked for accuracy from an individually conceived design or concept. In modern industry, the worker modifies his or her sense of accuracy, craftsmanship, and individuality within the constraints of standardization. Finally, in the traditional sense, skills were handed down from one generation to the next and were subject to individual idiosyncrasies. Modern industry makes a significant effort to standardize production and to develop methods increasing output.

The challenge in reorganizing the workplace rested, to a great degree, upon the internalization of the notion of what constituted "proper work patterns" by both unskilled and skilled labor. The consciousness of the worker required attention: the hands oiling the vast machining of the new industrial order would have to work at a steady and regular rate. This internal mentality, i.e., the psyche of the workers combined with the physical movements of that work had to be regulated and controlled. And it *would* be controlled by the instrumental logic of the new scientific rationality, the cornerstone of the modern industrial workplace. As an ultimate consequence, ends were emphasized over means, quantity over quality, efficiency over creativity, and production over human emotional needs. Functional music, the music of Muzak, would emerge as a powerful tool -- one of the major symbols of this new instrumental rationality.

The efforts of labor management through engineers and scientists were now directed to determine how even smaller amounts of labor time could produce even greater quantities of product. This, cyclically, led to even more research design, and manufacture of efficient methods and machinery. Control of the *labor* process was now clearly in the hands of management who justified this control by scientific rationality -- all in the name of efficiency.

The earliest time and motion studies of Frederick W. Taylor serve as one of the clearest examples where the goals of science and capitalism complement each other. Taylor was born in Germantown, Pennsylvania in 1856 and was educated in France, Germany and at Phillips Exeter Academy. In 1874 he was graduated from Harvard Law School. Poor eyesight forced him to abandon his law career and from 1874 to 1878 he was apprenticed as a pattern maker and machinist in a Philadelphia pump company. Remarkably, at his own insistence, Taylor was assigned as a manual laborer for the Midvale Steel Company in Philadelphia. He was promoted rapidly and became an engineer in 1884. One year earlier, after years of night study, he had received a mechanical engineering degree from the Stevens Institute of Technology in Hoboken, New Jersey. (The Stevens Institute was later to have Harold Burris-Meyer and Richard Cardinell on its faculty. They are credited, while associated with the Muzak Corporation, with ultimately discovering the concept of stimulus progression. And it was at the Stevens Institute in the late 1930's that the effect of functional music in reducing absenteeism was discovered. How curious that this one educational institution would be so inextricably linked to the most successful purveyors of functional music -- the Muzak Corporation.)

Taylor, who eventually was to obtain about 100 patents, systematically studied and measured shop procedures at Midvale. He developed a set of principles for manufacturing which was later recognized as the first empirically based system of "scientific" management, i.e., the "Taylor System" of time and motion. Taylor left Midvale in 1891 to establish a shop-management consultant firm but served for three years (1898-1901) exclusively as a consultant to the Bethlehem Steel Company. His book, published in 1911, titled the *Principles of Scientific Management* is regarded as a classic.

Taylor's views on scientific engineering accelerated the standardization of the labor process in two ways. First, the movement of every laborer was minutely studied and analyzed with a view towards eliminating waste and inefficiency. Second, Taylor's subsequent recommendations reappeared in the theories of industrial psychologists who assisted management in aiding workers in *adjusting* to this new environment and its increasing pressures. In one of the earliest texts on industrial psychology, Hugo Munsterberg's *Psychology and Industrial Efficiency* (1913), there is a direct intergration of the new discipline, industrial psychology, with Taylor's time and motion studies. (Munsterberg's book had been published the previous year in German: *Psychologie und wirtschafts leben.*) Psychologists should select the fittest person for each job, Munsterberg explains, and could assist in establishing working conditions that would obtain the greatest productivity from the workers. Thus, commerce and industry had placed at its disposal and service the findings from psychological experiments. Munsterberg urged his colleagues to go beyond the laboratory and the university, and to accompany him in remolding the work process. Many did. The early work was confined to the development and refinement of job selection exams, determining the right applicant, that is, the one with the mental abilities appropriate for the desired position.

Industrial management, as an academic discipline, was quick to gain acceptance and stature. Pittsburgh's Carnegie Tech in 1915 established a department of applied psychology. A Bureau of Salesmanship Research was soon created as an adjunct to the department. The Bureau was a privately financed organization which specialized in applying the methods of this new psychology to management problems. Funding was received from the Ford Motor Company, Goodrich Tire and Rubber, Westinghouse Electric, Heinz Foods, Prudential Insurance, and Carnegie Steel. (Interestingly, Ford and Prudential are among Muzak's current clients; Westinghouse owns Muzak). By all measures, projects examining the control of labor and productivity were well-funded.

It was the First World War, however, that dramatically raised the profile of industrial psychology; its increased role was felt both in the military and in the civilian business sector. The government, through the military's decision to test the intelligence and psychological attributes of doughboys, gave applied psychology (and later industrial psychology) a boost it might not have received in any other fashion. By 1920, fourteen months after the Armistice, hundreds of firms were purchasing standardized selection and intelligence tests, and a growing number of psychologists were hired as advisors to business and industry to help solve labor problems.

Next comes a crucial point. In order to gain respectability for the new discipline, applied psychologists doggedly held to the assertion that psychology could parallel the natural sciences in both theory and method. They believed that their discipline, not unlike the physical sciences, had a responsibility to go not only beyond the description and understanding of the various phenomena under scrutiny, but to predict and *control* them as well. There may or may not have been philosophical qualms about the intended purposes to which their findings would be put, but it was generally assumed that the refinement of these techniques to control people would be beneficial, an ameliorant for management. Control was not seen as repugnant or malicious, but as a necessity for the establishment of an environment where an employee would be happy and adjusted. A person's job and indeed his or her overall adaptation to the occupational milieu constituted the most significant adjustment he or she would have to make. Management's litany ran this way: success on the job meant more than material rewards, it meant social esteem and personal satisfaction. Here indeed was the "happiness" to go along with "life and liberty." The linkage of misery and work could indeed be broken. Conversely, the litany continues; an individual poorly adjusted in the job would have difficulty enjoying the remainder of life's activities. Talk about high stakes for the collective mental health of the nation, the literature in the field states even today that "happiness and effectiveness in nearly every other life-function is dependent upon satisfactory occupational adjustment." For the psychologist, the well-adjusted worker should have genuine enthusiasm for the job, would become deeply involved in it, and would feel that the work would make him or her a better person. It was assumed that any job could be interesting and enjoyable, and that only the well-adjusted worker would be able to uncover the rewards and challenges in work that the maladjusted worker would miss. The industrial psychologists would transform the mundane into the pleasant. Misery and the workplace would never again be synonymous.

Well-adjusted workers would be a boon for the industrial manager, too. What could be better for business than a labor force comprised of smiling, well-adjusted employees? Adjustment and diligence were viewed as reciprocal, mutually-supportive attributes by the psychologists. They discovered the fundamental linkage between happiness, which was derived from being well-adjusted and productive. The role played by industrial psychologists was a very important one in the nation's history. They assisted in assuaging the fears of the depressed and frightened business community at a time when there was a palpable threat of radical social unrest. A happy and well-adjusted labor force was not only possible, given the progress of research in industrial psychology, but a contented labor force would be more productive. Industry, therefore, would be more profitable. It fell now to trained industrial psychologists to analyze the workplace in order to make it as pleasant as possible. With the industrial revolution fully accomplished, it became the worker who was the problematic element in the production and profit-making process.

This change in the psychological definition of human beings as workers was, of course, aligned with the engineering and production changes of the new, highly industrialized society. The corporate managers in this new society were trained as engineers. (This is a role being played today by systems analysts as the industrial revolution continues.) These engineers conceived formulas and procedures, participated in corporate decisions, and developed elegant rationalizations and efficient methods -- always expressed in terms of cost vs. benefit and ends vs. means. The grand sum of these activities formed the most formal administrative structures and bureaucracy which characterize the modern, large corporation. From these activities emerged a well-defined and maintained line of authority, power, and communication.

To conclude this exploration of the first root cause of the Muzak Society, it is important to recognize that modern U.S.

management techniques have their genesis in the shift in focus on the part of the early engineers from the design of *things* to the control of *people*. These efforts to create a modern workforce involved two aspects. First, was the reorganization of the work activity for the laborer; this was "social engineering," or the overt attempt by management to exercise total control of the workplace. Second, there is "human engineering," or the control of *the individual* worker in the production process. Management therefore came to exercise control at both the social and individual levels; the two, of course, are bound together. Refinement of the techniques of social and human engineering lead to the fine science of labor management.

The scientists of labor management developed two approaches to the pesky problem of labor unrest. "Industrial relations" was one approach, "personnel management" the other. The former was determined to improve the welfare of workers to win their loyalty, and hence, cooperation. Personnel management was aimed at changing human beings by engineering the behavior of humans through the utilization of the newfangled tools of psychology and social psychology, all within an engineering context. Even by the end of the 1920's, industrial relations had become "human relations," the buzzword for converting what management perceived as a constant labor problem into an efficient, well-adjusted cog in the corporate mechanism. The challenge was clear-cut: to instill in employees the motives of selfless service and loyalty even to the extent of restricting individual aspirations and potential -- all to fit the corporately defined need and dimension.

Human relations, as a new weapon, was designed therefore to outflank the labor problem, which, viewed in the eyes of the industrialists was a concern of macrocosmic dimensions, i.e., the root cause of social instability. Rather than focusing on the worker, these studies stressed the idea that worker contentedness and productivity could be enhanced by ameliorating the external conditions of the worker's life. It was perceived that better housing, for example, would result in a more cooperative, efficient, and level-headed labor force.

"Personnel management," on the other hand, was the other set of techniques, procedures and growing body of knowledge employed to deal with the stubborn problem of labor. This was a direct approach to the exercise of control and was specifically concerned with the work situation -- in terms of both the individual worker and the *workers organized by task.* The focus of this scientific investigation was the control of the worker operating within the work situation itself. It was in this milieu that the corporate engineer made significant progress in the solution of the ongoing "problem" of labor. This was human engineering and a complement to industrial relations in that it was aimed at the adjustment of workers; and, it was accomplished *within* the workplace.

Human engineering then differs very little from other types of engineering. Human engineering consists of the prediction of behavior after careful observation, and the manipulation of the conditions necessary to produce a desired result. That result, of course, is increased profit. However, as stated before, it was the human element, rather than raw materials, that became the object of attention. Underlying this new social science was the assumption that every factor that influences human behavior could be observed, quantified, categorized, and ultimately controlled and manipulated.

Human engineering was the new causal mode of analysis which provided the foundation upon which the reorganization and restructuring of both business and industry were based; it was rational and positivistic. Moreover, this engineering perspective permeated the political-industrial complex to the extent that at one time during the Herbert Hoover administration (1928-1932), Hoover and the five CEO's of the largest corporations at that time (GM, Singer Sewing Machines, Dupont, GE, and Goodyear) were formerly classmates in engineering at MIT. Social order, and certainly order within the workplace, was now being rationally engineered by technicians. Part of the formulation for the Muzak Society had been laid.

Chapter 5

THE ELECTRIC REVOLUTION AND INDUSTRIAL SOUNDSCAPE

Silence . . . is a terrible thing.

Muzak Spokesman

The electric revolution expanded on many aspects of the Industrial Revolution and, on top of that, added some altogether new ones. Two entities heretofore unknown were introduced to the world: the realization of the packaging, storage, and retrieval of sound, and the removal of sound from its original performance context.

Spearheading the electric revolution were three unique sound inventions: the telephone, phonograph and the radio. Many of the basic discoveries leading to this revolution had already been made by 1850, e.g., the electric cell, the storage cell, dynamo, and the electric arc light. However, it was the very detailed *application* of this knowledge, that is, the practical creation of material goods, that occupied people's lives in the second half of the century. In this latter period the sound mechanisms of the phonograph record and the power mechanism of the electric power station came into existence. Initially, their full-blown commercial applications were seen as limited; necessary capital, typically from private sources, for the early primitive projects and prototypes was meager. It remained for the improvement of the dynamo by Werner Siemens and the alternator by Nikola Tesla that the now muted power of electricity would emerge as *the* significant catalyst for the further practical development of these new inventions.

With the telephone and the radio, sound was no longer tethered to its original point in physical space. With the phonograph, sound was no longer tethered to its initial point in time. This historically unprecedented removal of the restrictions in sound production, transportation, and retrieval is unique to modern technology. Up to the invention of the telephone by Alexander Graham Bell in 1876 and the development by Thomas Alva Edison of the phonograph in 1877, *homo sapiens* had heretofore heard sounds only as "originals," that is, they were perceived at one time and in one place only. Certainly the fascination and mystery of hearing one's echo is based on this being one of the very few occurrences when man can hear his own voice repeated. Sounds were directly associated with the individual or circumstance that produced them. The human voice could be sent only as far as one could shout, and the human intellect had devised acoustical devises whose sound product could travel only slightly farther, as with orchestral instruments and drums.

Sounds before the electric revolution were unique. Even though they may bear a resemblance to one another, and a trained ear could approximate the sound, the replication could never be exact. After the electric revolution, however, the equipment manufactured for the recording, storage, and transmission of sound could endlessly replicate it for the first time in history. And, not only can it exactly replicate it, it can expand on it and project it around the world or out into the galaxy. Sounds may now be packaged, placed on audio tape and/or phonogragh records and used by later generations. Sounds may be removed from their points of origin, transported great distances, duplicated a million times, and replicated at will. They have, in effect, been given independent status. Vocal sounds, as in song, are no longer related simply to the mouth and humanness, but may be heard anywhere in the environment. What has happened is that sound has been given a new status -- the status of an *object* and has lost that crucial attribute as an aspect of a specific *process*. Sounds -- spoken, sung, or performed on an instrument -- are no longer exclusively the result of communication between persons or of situational action. By the very nature of having the capacity to remove sounds from their point of origin, their meaning is transformed -- a crucial dimension to understanding the Muzak Society. This is because the sound itself, rather than the context in which it was performed, has long since in our conceptualization become the focal point.

To reiterate, in the electric revolution, sounds themselves can be divorced from the situation in which they first appeared; their *meaning* can be changed from one of process and action to that of object and tool.

This innovative treatment of sounds, as derived from technological advancement, is similar to the relationship of the worker to the labor process as created by the applied and industrial psychologists. In both instances, the meaning of the activity and the social interaction from which this meaning has been traditionally derived has been modified. Now *both* people and sound have been recast as objects -- their humanness subsumed as a means to an end. What these transmogrifications mean in reference to society and the creation of meaning by individuals is the focus of this polemic: the sounds in the Muzak Society are, of course, functional music. The location and specific social situation in which these sounds are used is the workplace, primarily, but also the shopping place, and the waiting place -- anywhere in which a palliative is needed to control things.

It is in the context of a historically deficient knowledge of the effects of sound on humans that the insights of R. Murray Schafer, a Canadian composer and music educator, take on added significance. Sounds have the ability to evoke emotional response as they are typically linked with human action and/or activity in nature. Likewise, a sound cannot exist without some form of movement occurring, e.g., the beating of a drum, a string vibrating, a cold and warm weather front colliding, etc. On this basis, Schafer developed a theory concerning the relationship of sound to power and authority. Schafer contends that loud noises evoke a sense of respect and sometimes fear. These loud sounds have traditionally been viewed as evidence or an expression of divine power. (Or in the case of Steven

Spielberg's *Close Encounters of the Third Kind,* at least extraterrestrial power. Recall the mother ship's reluctant but booming reply to the feeble entreaties of the earthlings.) Using careful observation from a number of cross cultural studies, Schafer concluded that this loud sound = power equation appears to have been transferred by man from sounds in nature, e.g., thunder, wind storms, the ocean, etc., to man-made objects capable of imitating (if not competing with) those sounds -- the pipe organ, festive church bells, the gong or tam-tam, and the bass drum or timpani. These sounds are really loud *noises,* but are labeled "sacred noise" due to their function, social context, and initial means of production. Sacred noise is to be distinguished from "nuisance noise" which has *none* of these attributes and requires, i.e., *demands,* abatement.

The industrial and electric revolutions redefined the relationship between the loud noises of nature and the deities, and the weaker "human" voices of industrial production. In the Age of Reason, paralleling the genesis of the Industrial Revolution, loud machine noise was granted a dispensation. Its loudness was rationalized -- all for progress. Previously, in the medieval monasteries, monks were granted similar dispensations to make occasional sacred noises on the chapel bell. Likewise, Johann Sebastian Bach was granted the freedom to make sacred noise on the pipe organ. The linkage of noise and power has never been altered in the human psyche. Loud noises cause wonderment; they have the power to startle. Sacred noise, which is the symbolic sound of divine power, descends first from God, to a minister or priest, and then, in our modern world, to the industrialist. Where there is the ability to make noise without censure or interference, there is power. Or, to put it another way, where noise in granted immunity from intervention or prohibition, as in Muzak's functional approach, power will be found.

Universally, the purpose of music in the workplace has been to aid the work effort. The timing of the work stroke, the setting of a steady pace and the easing of the monotony of repeated actions all seem to have fostered the development of music in work. The variety of musics which have been used to help the work effort is as diverse as human cultures. Throughout the world, solo songs and songs of working groups can be heard; music accompanies the countless vocations of both men and women. In the western world, the use of songs to accompany work is well-documented. Handmill songs, songs accompanying the preparation of textile material, weaving songs, water-drawing songs, songs tied to agricultural operations, plowing, planting, mowing, harvesting, and fruit-picking are all cited. Trade songs were found by ethnomusicologists to be characteristic of whole classes of artisans, and communal songs were used to lighten the load of men engaged in building, excavating, loading vehicles, or managing ships. Chanties were sung by sailors while weighing anchor, hoisting sails, raising masts or pumping water. This documentation, unfortunately, was based on observations published in the early Twentieth century. These then were some of the last descriptions of this music as it became lost to the ages for failure to record it. In many of these work settings, there was not even a written symbolic system by which the music could be preserved.

Certainly the closest contemporary Americans can fathom this musical tradition as described above is the traditional Black American worksongs sung by the few remaining chain gangs. These are traditional work songs, derived from West African origins, and are perceived as "heard action." Heard action refers to the song's subject matter, responsive form, improvisation, its direct link to the work at hand, and the tie it makes between sound and action. An important point to remember is that here, the music and labor are all one. There is no distinction between work and music -- the motor activity and music are bound together. While not entertainment, this music engages the workers and facilitates the completion of their collective task. Men laboring in groups produced song as a natural consequence of working, not in spite of hard laboring; music was simply part of the work ethic.

For work gangs, these songs were part of an old and familiar repertoire. A good song leader, as essential to the group as the singing preacher on Sunday, determined what song was needed at a given time; he knew how to sing it, too. As with any group, a hierarchy was in place: one's status in the work gang was the position one held in relation to the lead singer. A good leader stayed in "command" through his ability to improvise and create new songs. Many songs were heard for the first time literally minutes after the events which produced it took place.

Another important point to keep in mind is that by singing, the worker was able to transform song into the movement and force required by the work effort. The beat was the essential ingredient: the rhythm of the song had to match the task at hand. The leader, like a modern office manager, had to weigh the variables to ensure that his pace was neither too slow or too quick; he had to be able to sense when the workers could be pushed. This is, of course, a far cry from Muzak in the workplace. Here the music was developed through social interaction for the work of *that* day, *that* moment, *that* task. It was part of the laboring process. It was music created by the workers themselves and controlled by them; it was produced in their domain and defined by their conceptions of time.

The industrial workshop changed all this. It separated the workers from their work song. With the emergence of this new social and industrial ethic, work music lost its effect as a form of communication between people. A form of communication which had defined the rhythms of the work effort was now overwhelmed by the roar of machinery. The machinery of production, the power loom, the thresher, sewing machine, and typewriter all added new sounds and rhythms in the workplace overpowering human sounds. And there was no opposing this progress, despite the vast increase in noise. No one -- the unions, social reformers, physicians nor early psychologists saw the significance of the din in the workplace. (There was at least one isolated example of a naive awareness of the impact of loud noise on humans which was determined in 1890. "Boilermaker's disease" was a hearing impairment caused by the constant hammering and riveting required in the production of heavy machinery. Not one of a hundred boilermakers tested in 1890 had normal hearing.)

It is the *increase* in the volume of the sound that is the most salient characteristic of the Industrial Revolution. As industry grew, sounds grew with it. Noise is such a potent attention-getter. (It is interesting to speculate that if the machinery of the Industrial Revolution had been developed according to proper sound restraints, considering what we know now about the effects of loud noise on humans, the triumph of industrialization may have been delayed.)

This brings us to a redefinition of *imperialism.* If the extension of an empire and culture to places in the world removed from their point of origin is defined as *imperialism,* sound may also be described as imperialistic. Thanks to the electric revolution, when the power of sound is great enough to establish an acoustic profile dominating and masking other sounds in the environment, that may be said to be imperialistic. While a man with a booming voice might be said to be imperialistic, a man with a loudspeaker is exponentially more imperialistic because he and the machine can dominate more acoustical space. The revulsion of sensitive individuals to smart alecks with "ghetto blasters" is a natural reaction to having one's soundscape violated. Few people wish to lose that freedom of choice and be forced to become, however briefly, captive listeners. Another example: a person with a hand shovel is certainly not dominating the sound environment by his actions, but a person with a steam shovel is. It is one thing to have the ability to move more earth which imbues this tool with increased power and influence over its hand-held counterpart. It is certainly another to totally dominate the *soundscape* at the same time. In the case of the power shovel, the pairing of the physical and aural dominance is just too much: the sound assists in silencing opposition. Thus, in quasi-Newspeak, the ability to dominate is the ability to control. Those who are silenced are not heard; they become nonentities.

In the history of labor management, the application of recorded and broadcast music in the workplace as an implement of acoustical influence furthered an already active process of silencing the worker. As mentioned in Part I, the use of prerecorded and broadcast music in the workplace began in the 1930's. The picture was now nearing completion: a long evolution was about to bear fruit. The key variables in this evolution in the workplace were (1) the development of the technology to record, store, and transmit sound and (2) the refinement of a social psychology, called personnel relations, which was geared to assist workers in their rationalization of the demands made upon them in the workplace.

With war clouds gathering, interest in worker productivity and increased efficiency were rekindled. Concerted efforts were undertaken to carefully and now *scientifically* evaluate the psychological effects of music on the industrial worker.

The heritage of this new scientific inquiry can be traced to the Greeks. Employing the elegant logic of linear causality, as reflected in the scientific method, music became the *independent* variable. Music was thus studied as an independent entity, very removed, and *removable* from social interaction and all that that process entails. Music was now viewed in these studies as merely another sound in the workplace. It was seen as capable of eliciting a response in the *dependent* variable, here identified as individual productivity. Such a conception of music as external to the process of its creation and perception is indicative of the epistemology of the scientific method which seeks to categorize and separate, to determine cause and effect, to place things in neat, tidy boxes. Music, for the first time in history, was removed from human action and redefined as just one of the tools of production.

Studies on the relationship of music and behavior date from the 1880's. These early experiments found that music influenced blood pressure, pulse rate, and respiration. Subsequent studies up through the 1920's reinforced these early findings. Other studies showed that music increased metabolism and could modify or intensify mood in the respondents. These studies, however, were secondary to the research being done with "functional work music." Initially, these studies were concerned with the effect of music on muscular energy. It was found that music accompanying the work effort could (1) increase the intensity of sudden effort (2) extend the duration of sustained effort and (3) heighten the power of renewing it. The scope of these early studies was later expanded to include the relationship between music and attention span. The studies were done by Wyatt and Langdon, two British scientists. Specifically, theirs was the first, systematic evaluation of the effect of music on the performance of repetitive tasks. They measured the output of twelve young women engaged in the monotonous task of making paper firecrackers. They altered, as good ergonomists should, both the conditions of the labor and the types of music played for the women. Output increased with music, which was *broadcast* to the workers. While weak methodologically, Wyatt and Langdon were the first to observe the effect of *rhythm* on the workers -- the earliest finding supporting Muzak's later use of the stimulus progression technique. Interviews with workers also showed that the music tended to act as a palliative and silence worker grumbling:

> In some cases the rhythm was mentioned as an aid in production, as 'you try to work to the music especially when the time was quick' and 'a rather quick time makes you work quick.' In others, the music was said to 'make you better because you talked less,' or 'when on a bad job I thought more about the music than the job,' or 'the music helped you to take your mind off your troubles' and 'if on a bad job, the music most certainly helped you to forget and stop grumbling.'

Similar studies with similar results were undertaken in the U.S., and despite weaknesses in the methodology employed, the results were both widely disseminated and accepted by industrial pyschologists. The conclusion was that music enhances productivity in short-cycle, highly repetitive jobs, i.e., blue-collar, assembly line work. Later, the focus was shifted to the impact of music in white-collar settings.

Initially, the early studies in white-collar settings were inconclusive. Music *assisted* the work effort and was regarded by workers as beneficial, but it was here that the *choice* or programming of the music became the key variable. (Perhaps the lack of conclusiveness early on was related to the dearth of measurements regarding *qualitative* output as opposed to the blue-collar studies which were primarily concerned with quantitative results.)

Still, by 1939 Charles Diserens was able to develop four theories on why music had a favorable effect in productivity. In his *Psychology of Music*, he ascribed this phenomenon to:

(1) The regulation of movements involved in work by the rhythms of the music employed.

(2) The increased attention to work because of the music.

(3) A condition he described as a "more rapid repair" made under musical stimuli.

(4) The direct, physiological, and stimulating *value* of the music.

It is important to remember that these experiments were designed in such a way that the workers *received* the music as they worked. The music replaced the noise of machinery or filled the silence, which had replaced human, active voices. This music was tested and its effect measured based on a value system which eliminated the influence and interference of the workers.

Finally, it was with the results in hand that a number of companies became involved with furthering music in the workplace, Muzak the most prominent. They and some of the other companies had the capital necessary to investigate further the impact of music on workers in the labor process.

Controlling workers at their labor connected these firms to the compelling cultural value system that held that efficiency and productivity were to be achieved at any cost. In this manner, these companies participated in furthering the ideas of unfettered industrial growth and development.

Chapter 6

THE CASE OF THE CAPTIVE AUDITOR

"For some time he sat gazing stupidly at the paper. The telescreen had changed over to strident military music. It was curious that he seemed not merely to have lost the power of expressing himself, but even to have forgotten what it was that he had originally intended to say."

Orwell's, *1984*

We have seen that the roots of the Muzak Society lie in the product of two revolutions. The first is the need to control the labor force as an outgrowth of the Industrial Revolution and the second relates to music being treated as an object having been separated from its original context -- stored, retrieved, and reused -- a technology of the electric revolution. There is one other basis for the Muzak Society that requires our examination: its basis in law. There is legal precedent for subjecting captive auditors to background music. The case is the Public Utililties Commission of the District of Columbia vs. Pollak which was argued before the Supreme Court on March 3, 1952 and decided nearly three months later, on May 26th. The fundamental question was whether the U.S. Constitution precluded a bus and streetcar company (Capital Transit in Washington, D.C.) from receiving and broadcasting radio programming in its buses and streetcars (this was 1952).

This radio programming was supplied by Muzak and a number of its competitors to radio stations in various metropolitan areas in the country. "Transit radio," as it was called most frequently, was very popular from just after World War II through the mid-1950's. Though a product of the Muzak Corporation, it wasn't *the* Muzak we know today. Instead, it can be likened to those "easy-listening" formats, i.e., background music which is presently available in every radio market in the country.

The important point to remember is that this is the most celebrated case of a captive auditor attempting to establish his constitutional right not to be subjected to functional music. That's why, as one can imagine, the ultimate finding of the Court has such ramifications. While this saga has some Orwellian overtones, be assured that this is not fiction.

In March of 1948, Capital Transit began to experiment with a "music as you ride" campaign using radio programs received and amplified through speakers placed strategically throughout the bus and streetcar. Initially, only one streetcar and one bus were used for the pilot study. The equipment included the radio receiver and six speakers in each vehicle. The speakers were located so that the radio programming (the set was tuned to a single, contracted radio station) could be heard uniformly throughout the streetcar and bus. The contract called for the volume of sound to be adjusted so as not to interfere with the signals or announcements effecting vehicle operations or with conversations among passengers.

The vehicles were operated on various routes and at various hours. A poll of the passengers who were subjected to the programming indicated that 92 percent favored its continuance. As another part of the pilot study, Capital Transit studied other cities using transit radio. It was found that in October of 1949, the following number of vehicles were equipped similarly:

St.Louis	1,000
Cincinnati	475
Houston	270
Worcester (MA)	220
Tacoma (WA)	135
Evansville (IN)	110
Wilkes-Barre	100
Pittsburgh	75
Allentown (PA)	75
Huntington (WV)	55

. . . among others

Capital Transit subsequently entered into an agreement with Washington Transit Radio, Inc., a privately owned corporation also in the District of Columbia. Capital Transit, itself was a privately owned public utility corporation operating, because of the District's unique governance situation, *under a franchise from the United States Congress.* That authorization, dating from 1925, prohibited the establishment of any competitive street railway or bus line without the issuance of a certificate by the Commission to the effect that a new line would be necessary for the convenience of the public. Capital Transit, therefore, was a privately owned monoply sanctioned by the D.C. Public Utilities Commission which answered only to the Congress of the United States -- an important point which was explored by critics of the subsequent decision.

Capital Transit's agreement with Washington Transit Radio granted the latter the exclusive right to install, maintain, repair, and utilize radio reception equipment in Capital Transit's streetcars, buses, terminal facilities, waiting rooms, and division headquarters. Washington Transit Radio, in turn, agreed to contract with a broadcasting station for programs to be received no fewer than eight hours each day, Monday through Saturday. Washington Transit Radio secured the services of WWDC-FM, the station having met Capital Transit's terms: "The program content shall be of good quality and consonant with a high standard of public acceptance and responsibility, it being understood that all programs shall be carefully planned, edited and produced in accordance with accepted practices . . ." By February 1949, more than twenty installations had been made. Protests came immediately. Accounts at the time describe these protests as "vigorous," with some passengers asserting that their constitutional rights had been violated. By late October of 1949 there would be 212 installations. A total of 1,500 installations were planned over a five-year period, with an automatic renewal clause written into the original contract.

The protests were so vigorous that the Commission decided to hold hearings. These proceedings began in July 1949. The

Commission wished to determine whether the installation and use of such receivers was consistent with "public convenience, comfort, and safety." Washington Transit Radio appeared before the Commission as did the Capital Transit passengers who protested. The Commission concluded that the installation and use of radios in streetcars and buses was *not* inconsistent, etc., etc., and dismissed the investigation. Furthermore, it denied reconsideration. The irate passengers appealed to the United States District Court. Three views were heard: that of Capital Transit, Washington Transit Radio, and the passengers. The passengers lost again. Next stop, the Court of Appeals. This court partially *reversed* the judgment of the District Court and gave instructions to vacate the Commissions order. It remanded the case for further proceeding at the District Court level. Curiously, it was the commercials and announcements broadcast by Washington Transit Radio that drew the wrath of the Court:

> In our opinion Transit's broadcasts deprive objecting passengers of liberty without due process of law. Service that violates constitutional rights is not reasonable service. If follows that the commission erred as a matter of law in finding that Transit's broadcasts are not inconsistent with public convenience, in failing to find that they are unreasonable, and in failing to stop them.
>
> This decision applies to 'commercials' and to 'announcements.' We are not now called upon to decide whether occasional broadcasts of music alone would infringe constitutional rights.

With the Court of Appeals denying a rehearing, the Commission, Captial Transit, and Washington Transit Radio petitioned the Supreme Court. Once the Supreme Court decided to hear the case, Pollak and Martin, the protesting passengers, cross petitioned. They sought to prohibit Capital Transit from receiving and amplifying in its vehicles not only the commercials and announcements but the balance of the programming, i.e., the music. The Supreme Court cited both the novelty and practical importance of the case and decided to combine the petition and cross petition into one case.

In a critical ruling, the Court decided that its proceedings were restricted to the facts obtained by the Public Utilities Commission in the latter's previous hearing since they appeared not to be "unreasonable, arbitrary, or capricious." Therefore, having matters restricted to a consideration of only the public convenience, comfort, and safety aspects, Justice Harold Burton, writing for the Court, cited huge amounts of testimony verbatim from the initial hearing. For example, Justice Burton noted that the Commission said that,

> From the testimony of record, the conclusion is inescapable that radio reception in streetcars and busses [*sic*] is not an obstacle to safety of operation. Further, it is evident that public comfort and convenience is not impaired and that, in fact, through the creation of better will among passengers, it tends to improve the conditions under which the public ride.

Continuing in this paternalistic, Big Brother vein, Justice Burton accepted the Commission's claim citing its conclusion that public comfort and convenience were *enhanced* by the radio broadcasts. For evidence he noted the opinions of the streetcar and bus operators to the effect that the "music on the vehicles had a tendency to keep the passengers in a better mood, and that it simplified transit operations." Moreover, the radio broadcasts were seen not to have been the cause of any accidents. Justice Burton then plopped into the record additional Commission testimony:

> A public opinion survey was conducted by Edward G. Doody and Company, from October 11, 1949, to October 17, 1949, in order to determine the attitude of Capital Transit Company customers toward transit radio. This survey employed the rules of random selection and was confined to interviews aboard radio-equipped vehicles.

> The principal results obtained through the survey, as presented in this record, were as follows:
>
> Of those interviewed, 93.4 percent were not opposed; that is, 76.3 were in favor, 13.9 said they didn't care, and 3.2 said they didn't know; 6.6 percent were not in favor, but when asked the question 'Well, even though you don't care for such programs personally, would you object if the majority of passengers wanted busses [*sic*] and streetcars equipped with radio receivers,' 3.6 said they would not object or oppose the majority will. Thus, a balance of three percent of those interviewed were firmly opposed to the use of radios in transit vehicles.

Burton found no fault therefore with the Commission's dismissing the original hearings, noting that apart from the constitutional issues, the Commission was in accord with its prescribed statutory procedure and within the discretion properly vested in that body by the Congress. What about the issues? Here the opinion of the Court takes a curious, if predictable, turn. Apparently not understanding music's pervasive nature and using the profit motive to subvert some passenger's First Amendment rights in favor of the Transit Company, Burton observed that the radio service is a "new income-producing incident to the operation of railway properties." (The profit arose from the rental of facilities for advertising purposes.) This aspect of the enterprise appeared to bear some relation in Burton's thinking to the long-established and practice of "renting space for visual advertising on the inside and outside" of the vehicles.

Burton saw D.C. Transit acting in a good-faith fashion by seeking to improve its public relations. He found that the contractual arrangement between Transit Radio and D.C. Transit was being carried out. Ninety percent of the radio time was indeed being used for purposes other than commercials and announcements. The breakdown was 90 percent music, 5 percent news, weather reports and matters of civic interest, and 5 percent commercial advertising.

Still, Burton could not ignore the Commission's consideration of the intensity and nature of the passenger's objections. Those objections raised by the individuals who attended the hearings were based upon the broadcasts interfering with their thinking, reading, or chatting with other passengers. Others, more vociferous in their objections, indicated that the broadcasts would lead to thought-control; the noise was disturbing; the commercial messages, announcements, and time checks were annoying; the music was of the poorest class; the practice deprived their property rights without due process; their health was being impaired; finally, they asserted that there was *indeed* a safety problem due to the effect of the radio on the vehicle operators.

It was in the applicability of the First and Fifth Amendments ("Congress shall make no law . . . abridging the freedom of speech . . . ; no person shall . . . be deprived of life, liberty, or property without due process of law; . . .") that the ruling takes on a more curious aspect. First, it was held by the Court that the action of Capital Transit in installing and operating the radio system and the action of the Public Utilities Commission in dismissing its own investigation of the practice, sufficiently involved the Federal Government in responsibility for the programming to make the "First and Fifth Amendments to the Constitution of the United States applicable to this radio service." These amendments, Burton noted, "apply to and restrict only the Federal Government and not private persons." Having thus indicated that the Federal Government indeed had the right to examine the First and Fifth Amendments applicable to the case, Burton proceeded to find no violation of these amendments.

In regard to the First Amendment, Pollak and Martin, the protesting passengers, contended that the programming interfered with their freedom of conversation and that of other passengers by making it necessary for them to compete against the programs in order to be heard. The Commission dismissed this indicating that the programs did not interfere "substantially" with the converstions of passengers or with the rights of communication constitutionally protected in public places. Burton also suggested that there is an implication that the First Amendment guarantees a freedom to listen only to such "points of view" as the listener wishes to hear. But Burton noted that Pollack and Martin had not pressed this claim, that there was "no issue of that kind before us," and that the programs had not been used for "objectionable propaganda." The Court found that the inclusion in the programming of a few announcements "explanatory and commendatory" of Capital Transit's *own services* does not sustain such an objection, if indeed it had been made.

As for the Fifth Amendment, the ruling was the same: no violation. The protesting passengers had proven their point in the Court of Appeals that the programming was an invasion of their constitutional rights of privacy. Burton not only overturned this, he ridiculed it. "This claim is that no matter how much Capital Transit may wish to use radio in its vehicles as part of its service to its passengers and as a source of income, no matter how much the great majority of its passengers may desire radio in those vehicles, and however positively the Commission, on substantial evidence, may conclude that such use of radio does not interfere with the convenience, comfort, and safety of the service but tends to improve it, yet if one passenger objects to the programs as an invasion of his constitutional right of privacy, the use of radio on the vehicles must be discontinued." Burton wasn't through. He asserted that Pollak's and Martin's position wrongly assumes that the Fifth Amendment secures to each passenger on a public vehicle regulated by the Federal Government a right of privacy substantially equal to the privacy to which he is entitled in his own home. Having begged the question, the Justice answered it. "However complete his privacy may be at home, it is substantially limited by the rights of others when its possessor travels on a public thoroughfare or rides in a public conveyance." Streetcars and buses, the Court noted, are subject to the immediate control of their owner and operator, and by their dedication to public service, they are for the common use of all of their passengers; the Federal Government in its regulation of them is not only entitled, but is required, to take into consideration the interest of all concerned. (The logic here is elegant but nonetheless incorrect and about 180 degrees from our thinking in the last quarter of the century. D.C. Transit was a privately owned monopoly sanctioned by the Federal Government. As will be pointed out, many riders have no alternative other than to ride this public conveyance. Their "electing" to ride the buses and streetcars -- and, again, for many there is *no* alternative, means, if one follows Burton's logic, that they surrender a substantial portion of their most personal liberties all in the name of majority will and the profit motive.)

The Court continued by pointing out that there are mutual limitations upon the conduct of those riding public vehicles including the vehicle owner. These constraints relate to operating schedules, the location of streetcar and bus stops, as well as policies relating to the desirability or nature of radio programs in the vehicles. Where a regulatory body has jurisdiction, the Court continued, it will be sustained in its protection of activities in public places when those activities do not interfere with (and here we go again) the "general public convenience, comfort and safety." The Public Utilities Commission's handling of the matter in terms of substantive and procedural due process, having not been arbitrarily or capriciously exercised, was supported.

Pollak and Martin were then chided one additional time. The Court held that the petition of Pollack and Martin, if supported, would permit an objector, with a status no different from that of other passengers, to override not only the "preference of the majority of the passengers" but also the considered judgment of the "federally authorized Public Utilities Commission" which had held hearings and had come to a justifiable conclusion that the policies of the owner and operator did not interfere with public convenience, comfort, and safety."

In closing, Justice Burton, writing for the Court, made it clear that the court was not expressing any opinion as to the *desirability* of radio programs in public vehicles. "That is a matter between Capital Transit, the public, and the Public Utilities Commission." Burton then used an analogy to back this position by stating that the situation is not unlike that which arises when a utility makes a change in schedule in the interest of the majority of the passengers against the "vigorous protests of the few who are inconvenienced by the change." If that weren't enough, Burton pointed out that the Court of Appeals had refrained from considering the constitutionality of the receiving and amplifying of occasional broadcasts of music alone in public vehicles. This was another point made by Pollak and Martin in their petition. However, the results were the same with Burton decreeing "in view of our holding that the programs before us, containing music, commercial advertising and other announcements are constitutionally permissible, it is clear that programs limited to a like type of music alone would not be less so." With that, the Supreme Court, by a vote of six to two, reversed the judgment of the Court of Appeals. (Justice Frankfurter did not take part in the decision for reasons stated below.)

Two justices dissented: Black and Douglas. Black concurred with the majority except on the amendment question. He was of the opinion that subjecting Capital Transit's passengers to the broadcasting of news, public speeches, views or propaganda of any kind and by any means would violate that provision. The music portion of the programming, interestingly, did not concern him.

Justice Frankfurter's reaction to this case was curiously disappointing. Indicating that his feelings were so strongly engaged as a victim of the practice in question, he decided that he'd better not participate in judicial judgment upon it. While his disqualifying himself may have been a commendable act, it was left to Justice Douglas alone to champion the constitutional rights of the unwilling listener. What Frankfurter *might* have said would have very likely been interesting, if not controversial; he was already on record as having asserted that the captive auditor deserved constitutional protection from "aural aggressions."

Justice Douglas was eloquent in his dissent. His view was that the case boiled down to the meaning of liberty as used in the Fifth Amendment. Liberty in the constitutional sense, to Douglas, meant more than freedom from unlawful governmental restraint; it includes privacy as well, if it is to be a repository of freedom. Douglas followed this with the classic line, "The right to be let alone is indeed the beginning of all freedom." Part of Douglas' view in upholding the sanctity of privacy rested in the prohibition of the Fourth Amendment against unreasonable searches and seizures. This amendment guarantees that a man's home is his castle and is beyond invasion by inquisitive or officious persons. While a man loses that privacy when he goes into the street or enters public places, he still retains certain "immunities" from controls bearing on his privacy. He may not be compelled against his will to attend a religious service; he may not be made to accept one political or philosophical creed as against another. The freedoms guaranteed by the First Amendment give more, in Justice Douglas' thinking, than the privilege to worship, to write, to speak as one chooses; they give freedom *not* to do nor to act as the government chooses. The First Amendment in its respect for the conscience of the individual honors the *sanctity of thought and belief.* To think as one chooses, to believe what one wishes are important aspects of this constitutional right to be let alone.

Douglas was unhappy with the Court's narrow interpretation of the Fifth Amendment. He believed that Public Utilities Commission vs. Pollak involved a case of coercion to make people listen. He turns the tables on Burton by citing the public nature of the situation as opposed to the free choice that individuals might have in the home. "The listeners are, of course, in a public place. They are on streetcars [and buses] traveling to and from home. In one sense, it can be said that those who ride the streetcars [and buses] do so voluntarily." Yet, of course, in a practical sense (and because of the monopoly enjoyed by D.C. Transit) these individuals were forced to ride since this type of transportation is essential for many. "Compulsion which comes from circumstances can be as real as compulsion which comes from a command."

To our thinking in the late 1980's, the audience in those streetcars and buses in this case was indeed a captive one. The transportation was used by these people, as today, as a matter of necessity, not of choice. An individual who is in a public vehicle cannot complain about the crowd noise or the cacophony of many voices; in that regard, anyone who enters a public place sacrifices some of his privacy. Douglas' protest was against the invasion of his privacy *"over and beyond the risks of travel."* By "risk," Douglas means "circumstances."

The government or enterprises sanctioned by the government may use the media on public vehicles for many purposes. One would trust that these purposes would be cultural, not political. But, as far as the right of privacy is concerned, the purpose makes no difference. One bureaucrat's selection may be as offensive to some as it is calming to others, Douglas' dissent continues. The news commentator reporting the events of the day may give a slant to the news that might hearten the bureaucrat, but would rile the captive auditor. The political philosophy which one radio speaker exudes may be thought by the official who develops the bus programs to be best for the welfare of the people. But the individual listening to it on the way to work may construe it as marking the destruction of the Republic. An offensive program can be turned off; stations can be changed. Disquieting or unpleasant programs in restaurants can be avoided by leaving the premises. But captive auditors on the bus have no choice but to sit and listen -- or sit and try *not* to listen.

People, Douglas concluded, who are forced to listen to another's ideas fall into the hands of the propagandist. Today it is a business enterprise, tomorrow it may be programming by a dominant political or religious group. There is potential vice in the situation, Douglas noted. Once privacy is invaded, privacy is gone. Once a person is forced to submit to one type of program, he can be forced to submit to another. If liberty is to flourish, government should never be *allowed* to force people to listen to any program. The right of privacy should include the right to select from competing entertainments, propaganda, and political philosophies. Finally,

> If people are let alone in those choices, the right of privacy will pay dividends in character and integrity. The strength of our system is in the dignity, the resourcefulness and the independence of our people. Our confidence is in their ability as individuals to make the wisest choice. That system cannot flourish if regimentation takes hold. The right of privacy, today violated, is a powerful deterrent to anyone who would control men's minds.

There is, of course, a matter of high principle in this case. This needs to be stated since the toughest obstacle to be removed in dealing with this subject in all earnestness, and with the Muzak Society as a whole, is the much encountered feeling that the whole matter, whatever its wrongs, is basically trivial -- much ado about nothing. The origin of this feeling is associative rather than logical; it fallaciously evaluates the interests invaded by forced listening in terms of the incontrovertible, immutable triviality of the music that the captive audience must listen to. Subjecting individuals hour after hour, day after day, to this forced feeding of trivial fare, is *not in itself a trivial matter*. To insist, by the effective application of coercion, that an individual's right to use and expend his or her own faculties stops short of the interests of others to endure irrefutable banality, is not itself banal, but instead a sinister symbol of the conflict between the independence of the minds of people and the desire to turn a profit.

In 1953, the *New Yorker*, long a front line fighter against audience captivity, protested the use of forced listening on buses in Yonkers. Alluding to the Washington case, the writer conceded that the captor had "the Supreme Court behind him." Well, yes and no. At the very least, the Court held that the objecting auditors could not find their deliverance in *constitutional* rights. This is frightening enough, but it does not amount to a general approval or sanctioning of coerced listening, or worse yet, to the establishment of the rights of the captor against those of the trapped auditors. Other avenues of protest were used back in the 50's and are still available to workers, riders, and shoppers today -- letters to the editor, complaints to the corporate headquarters, appeals to legislatures, councils, and commissions, etc. Where constitutional protection has failed, other modes of attack have become even more important. The central question in this case is still open and remains open today: "Do we want this thing among us?" It is certain that the Supreme Court won't decide that for us.

Finally, as for the Commission vs. Pollak, the facts are clear. A private transit company with the backing of public authority and holding a virtual monopoly implemented, in effect, public policy. A person has to ride the buses of the one company because the government authority says they are to be the only buses to run. (Running on common thoroughfares existing legally as public easements and maintained by public funds.) A monopoly, in a free enterprise setting, means the absence of an alternative to the customer; the government grants transportation monopolies -- transportation and communication being the second of the great functions of the State according to political scientists. Where audience captivity exists, the Public Utilities Commission, acting as a government organ and charged with the responsibility of policing the power of a monopoly, has acquiesced in the exercise of that power to compel listening to the bus radio.

Forced listening, as in this case, or by means of an employer placing speakers in the workplace, attacks the mind's integrity with a new directness. Assaults such as these subject the mind to slow starvation; the stimulus is chock-full of empty calories and few vitamins. It leads to the frustration of the mind and its eventual atrophy by forbidding its exercise in expression. It was reserved for our time, the Muzak Society, to bring it all together: the elements of the industrial and electric revolutions and a basis in the law, or the lack of an insight into the law, by the judiciary.

Muzak and its competitors have authored a technique that pushes more deeply, though no more painfully, into the minds of the unwilling than was thought possible by our forefathers' primitive consideration of censorship and suppression. A sound, just a little too loud and insistent to be ignored, in a place where a person *must be,* exacts a price for living a normal life in today's society. It is this submission to this daily intrusion of whatever cunning engineers think we require that constitutes conditioning and tampering with our minds. This is a deliberate attack on the central citadel of human personality. This discernment of what it is that is being attacked *should* lead us to seriously condemn the whole enterprise.

Man is a rational animal. We know this because he uses and understands language. Speech then is a serious matter, for it is speech that makes him manifest. Few attacks on the rationality of Man could strike with more power than to degrade him to the level of collectivized object of speech, powerless to both escape and answer. Much has been said and written on the relation of "freedom of speech" and "freedom from unwanted speech." Does the former include the latter? Clearly the claim to freedom from unwanted speech rests on a high moral plane and upon convictions held of human dignity very similar to, if not identical with, those historically brought forward in support of freedom of speech in the usual sense. Forced listening in the Muzak Society destroys and denies, practically and symbolically, the unrestrained interplay and competition between ideas which is an assumed ambiance of the freedom to communicate. It contradicts, in addition, what some would regard as a deeper, more fundamental law and that is the respect that should be held for each person as a unique user of the language, i.e., a unique user of communication, both verbal and nonverbal. Respect, not unlike liberty, is indivisible. A society which subjects its members in wanton contempt by treating their *listening* as an object cannot long hold the view that their verbal and nonverbal utterances deserve respect, too.

One cannot read Douglas' dissent in the reviews of the Commission vs. Pollak case without feeling that, regardless of the merits of the constitutional issues, here speaks a voice consonant with the best our culture has had to say about human dignity and the right to be let alone. It is otherwise embarrassing to admit to the foreign visitor that audience captivity in a variety of settings is not only perfectly legal, but is somehow fully in accord with those other ideals and practices by which we are adjudged in the world.

A few defenses of this practice have been put forward. One suggests that workers, riders, and shoppers don't really have to pay attention but may withdraw their minds at will, the whole thing, after all, being "psychological." Such a defense is fallacious when one considers the energy marshalled by Muzak and its competitors who have taken the resources of societal pressure, modern technology, and applied psychology to the precise end of making the withdrawal of subliminal awareness nearly impossible.

Some have asserted that forced listening is no worse than billboard signs on the highway, advertising on buses, or signs in taxicabs. One can avert the eyes but not the ears.

Now to the argument that workers actually like Muzak and functional music of its type. Surveys are not the last word in this matter, whatever the outcome, particualarly when Muzak conducts the survey. If our nation is committed to anything, it is to the placing of some interests beyond the reach of majority preference. Moreover, there is a difference between merely liking something and insisting on what you like at whatever cost to others. No company dealing with functional music has ever asked the question, "Even if you enjoy Muzak, as far as your own tastes go, do you want to continue to have it even if a good many of your colleagues are deeply outraged by it?" It is hardly complimentary to a civilized populace to assume that answer would be in the affirmative -- and hardly hopeful for the actual existence of those feelings of respect for others which we would like to think our society embodies. Do we have enough faith that the great majority would not wish to grasp this palliative at the expense of others' objection and anguish?

There is the assertion that a good deal of noise, verbal and nonverbal, is inescapably incidental if not essential to the workplace, and, after all, isn't Muzak at best masking it, or at worst, just one more sound? But Muzak is *not* incidental to the workplace and is *not* an essential by-product of workers' actions. Privacy and freedom from distraction are indeed rare in modern life, and to spoil what remains of them is hence even more injurious.

Social action is not just action, but symbolic as well. Captive audiences are a fact of life due to Muzak's general acceptance. It has then a symbolic meaning: where it exists and prevails, it is something everyone accepts as a standard, if not prominent feature of our life. We have seen that the Supreme Court has validated this concept against constitutional attack. We have acquiesced to it. Too bad. Because it appears that the mental and spiritual integrity of the citizen will not survive if it gets in the line of march for profit. Functional music treats people as a means rather than as an end; as a commodity rather than as a person. How our society can accommodate as normative behavior a pattern of action associated with totalitarian societies, is a compelling question.

General George Squier

General George Squier as chief of the U.S. Army Signal Corps. This brilliant military man and inventor had an entrepreneurial bent also. He developed the name for his new product in the 1930's by combining "music" with another trade name, Kodak; thus, Muzak.

U.S. Army Photo

Frederick W. Taylor

Frederick W. Taylor, the time and motion expert. His book, Principles of Scientific Management published in 1911, resulted from studying shop procedures in the steel industry.

UPI/Bettman Newsphoto

Justice Harold Burton

Justice Harold Burton, former mayor of Cleveland and U.S. Senator, wrote for the majority in the Supreme Court decision of the Public Utilities Commission of the District of Columbia v. Pollak in 1952. Pollak and fellow passengers had fought being subjected to broadcasts by Transit Radio in streetcars and buses in Washington, D.C. They lost.

UPI/Bettman Newsphoto

Justice William O. Douglas

Justice William O. Douglas succeeded Louis D. Brandeis as an Associate Justice of the U.S. Supreme Court. He agreed with the captive auditors in the Commission v. Pollak and cited his predecessor, Brandeis, by reaffirming that "the right to be let alone is indeed the beginning of all freedom".

UPI/Bettman Newsphoto

William Benton

William Benton bought Muzak from Warner Brothers in 1939. He had a distinguished career as an advertising executive, entrepreneur, university admimistrator, and public servant. As president, and later, chairman of the board, he brought Muzak into the Oval office, expanded its franchise system, and successfully reached accords with the America Federation of Musicians and ASCAP.

UPI/Bettman Newsphoto

James C. Petrillo

James C. Petrillo, czar of the Musician's Union and formidable foe of Muzak. During his controversial career, Petrillo led strikes against CBS and RCA, rejected President Roosevelt's plea for progress in a related labor dispute, and was charged (and acquitted) of violating the Lea Act, which Congress had enacted to curb broad union powers.

UPI/Bettman Newsphoto

Jack Kent Cooke

Jack Kent Cooke, real estate tycoon and owner of the Los Angeles Lakers, Los Angeles Forum, and Washington Redskins. He bought Muzak from the Wrather Corporation in 1972 to become part of the Teleprompter Corporation. He held the company for nine years selling it to Westinghouse and its Group W operations.

UPI/Bettman Newsphoto

PART III

MUZAK HATH CHARMS

Muzak is my favorite kind of music. I like anything on Muzak -- it's so listenable. They should have it on MTV.

Andy Warhol, in *Newsweek,* 1984

Chapter 7

Muzak: The Corporate Entity

Noting its use in both hospitals and funeral parlors, one observer said, "It's with us from start to finish now, from the womb to the tomb."

Nation's Business, 1950

The history of the Muzak Corporation makes an interesting chronicle of classic entrepreneurship. Following the creation of Wired Radio, Inc., a subsidiary of the North American Company, the parent company acquired a music publishing company which became Associated Music Publishers, Inc. The plan was now in place. The North American Company had thus bought General Squier's scheme to employ electric power lines to transmit news programs, music, lectures, general entertainment, and advertising directly into private homes. Associated Music Publishers, the other subsidiary, quickly bought the rights to a large number of classical and semi classical compositions which allowed the company to focus on prerecorded programming, since live talent had proven to be economically unfeasible even at this early date, 1932.

The first Muzak transmission originated from a power station owned by the Cleveland Illuminating Company, also a North American subsidiary, and was sent to subscribers in Cleveland's Lakewood section. By the end of 1934, Muzak had begun to transmit a new kind of music -- "functional" music to hotels and restaurants. Telephone lines now were being used instead of electric lines, and, to insure the fidelity of the sound, the recordings were made at 33-1/3 r.p.m., vertically engraved. These were the forerunners of the LP's that would not become commercially available until after World War II. These Muzak recordings were also the first to be pressed in vinylite, the latter being less prone to scratching than the shellac recordings.

Muzak's first true commercial operations began in New York City on March 6, 1936. The most prominent clubs, e.g., the Stork Club, were the first to subscribe to the new service. While many hotels and restaurants had "Music by Muzak" soon thereafter, commercial and industrial research continued in both the areas of sound technology, and psychological studies of the human reaction to the sound. Two discoveries were made. First, music used for functional purposes must be rational lest it become monotonous. The second discovery was that *programming* was essential to the effectiveness of functional music; in that manner, under planned conditions, productivity in work areas could be stepped up.

The success of Muzak in New York spurred the corporation to create a franchise system. The earliest franchises were in Detroit, Los Angeles, Boston, Washington, Philadelphia, and Buffalo. Each was operated under the strict agreement that programs were to be played without variation as planned and programmed by the Muzak Corporation.

Meanwhile, back in New York, *Newsweek* in March 1939 reported that Muzak had built up a clientele of 360 restaurateurs and had recently offered a new feature, apartment house receiving sets that rented from $3.50 to $5.00 a month bringing not only Muzak, but staticless reception from four commercial New York stations: WABC, WEAF, WJZ, and WOR. Muzak was still sticking to its original idea of piping music into individual residences. However, the cost for private homes was still prohibitive: $25 to $40 per month and only thirty well-to-do clients had, by early 1939, subscribed to this service.

Later that year, Muzak and the Associated Music Publishers were sold by Warner Brothers, who had owned the company for a year, to a business group headed by William Benton. The group expanded the number of Muzak franchises and concentrated on developing more sophisticated marketing techniques.

Business Week, September 14, 1940 described a prewar Muzak on the move, if a bit unfocused and offering a different set of services than we're accustomed to nearly fifty years later. The business magazine was interested in Muzak's serving Manhattan apartment houses with music piped over telephone wires and received via an "injecter box making it possible for tenants to get Muzak's program 17-1/2 hours a day. The "injecter boxes" (sounds a bit like the modern-day satellite TV descramblers) cost the landlords from $25 on up depending on the difficulty of installation. Sixty apartment houses were subscribing by mid-1940 and a number of others were dangling it as bait for advertising purposes. Muzak called this service to apartments the "Green Network." Since early 1939, a "Red Network" had served bars and short-order grills unable to afford the premium "Purple Network." The Red Network allowed advertising, lowering its price to subscribers to a mere $15 a month. The Purple, in contrast, cost $35 on up, *Business Week* reported. Advertising on the Red Network was limited to 15 seconds every 15 minutes.

Then, as now, there was rigid scheduling of the programming. It was not however the fifteen minutes on, fifteen minutes off, stimulus progression technique now employed by Muzak. Instead, there were eleven minutes of music and three minutes of silence from 10 a.m. to 3:30 a.m., Muzak's "broadcast" day. "Light" music was played until 3 p.m. when congas and rhumbas took over through the cocktail bour. Viennese waltzes were played for dinner. Dance arrangements were not played before 9:30 p.m. and no vocals before 11 p.m. Major sports events were sometimes broadcast on the Red Network, and subscribers to the Purple could request special selections. Most frequently requested after nearly a year of operation were a "wedding sequence" (*Lohengrin,* Wagner; *Midsummer Night's Dream,* Mendelssohn) and tunes on the order of *I Love You Truly* and *Happy Birthday.*" The latter was played an average of five times a day, and the all-time high was thirty-four times. The wedding sequence was requested twenty-seven times one day in June, 1940. These came over separate lines into party rooms while the hotel or restaurant itself was receiving regular programming. *Business Week* noted that there were few individual patrons, and, admittedly, business was slow at the time of the article. But Benton's impact was already being felt: starting in October, Muzak had lined up enough orders to plan one installation a day. And, in addition to carrying the speeches of Churchill and Roosevelt, Muzak planned to carry that fall's election returns.

One city missing from Muzak's list in its attempts at franchising was Chicago, *Business Week* noted. Here trouble was brewing and it would remain a stormy situation until 1950. Muzak's conspicuous absence from Chicago was due to James C. Petrillo, president of the American Federation of Musicians and a long-time foe of any type of canned music. Chicago was Petrillo's turf, and while New York and other locals had come to terms begrudgingly with Muzak, Chicago stood firm. In all but Chicago, Muzak and its franchise holders had signed agreements with the A.F. of M. locals guaranteeing not to sell its services in restaurants where its installation would mean the dismissal of musicians or the reduction in their playing time. Despite the outward amity, musicians were not happy with Muzak's growth since it paid only union scale on its recording dates rather than the higher rates commanded by name bands in performing radio, recording, and dance hall bookings. The union scale was only prudent business. Not until January, 1940 had Muzak shown a profit and there must have been some concern on Benton's part when his group bought the operation that the gamble would ultimately pay off.

As for the leader of the new owners, William Benton was born on April 1, 1900 in Minneapolis, the elder son of a Congregational minister. His mother was active in the progressive education movement. Benton was sent to the Shattuck Military School in Faribault, Minnesota and graduated from Yale in 1921, as had his father and grandfather. After a short stint with the National Cash Register Company, he became a copywriter for the advertising firm of Lord and

Thomas. His climb was meteoric and within five years he had become assistant manager of the agency and moved to Chicago. Earning $25,000 a year in 1929, he announced his plans to start his own agency. Lord and Thomas countered by offering $50,000 a year. Still, he quit, and with Chester Bowles (later to become governor of Connecticut) opened the Benton and Bowles Advertising Agency in November, 1929 -- hardly a propitious time to go it alone. By 1932 General Foods had entrusted seven major accounts to the firm making it one of the leading advertising agencies in the country. Their innovation? They were one of the first to use radio as an advertising medium. Benton and Bowles produced Maxwell House's *Showboat*, Palmolive's *Beauty Box* and *Gangbusters*, and Fred Allen's *Town Hall Tonight*. By 1935 Benton moved from the presidency to the board chairmanship. His company was grossing 18-million dollars a year by 1936, whereupon, at the height of the depression, he retired to become vice president of the University of Chicago. There he joined Robert Hutchins, who like Bowles was a Yale graduate. Hutchins as president and Benton as vice president teamed up to pioneer educational radio and movies. Benton's radio program, *The University Round Table* won several awards including a Peabody in 1944.

In 1943 the University of Chicago acquired the Encyclopedia Britannica from Sears with Benton providing the working capital to help close the transaction. For his efforts, he was named board chairman of Britannica's English and North American companies.

Benton combined his interests in the media with politics and public service. In 1939, the same year he led the group buying Muzak from Warner Brothers, he was an adviser to Nelson Rockefeller, who was then coordinator of Inter-American Affairs. In 1942, one year after becoming the sole owner of Muzak, Benton was appointed vice chairman of the Committee on Economic Development, a nonprofit organization he helped to found. In 1945 he became Assistant Secretary of State for Public Affairs, and, as such, vigorously promoted the Voice of

America and the use of radio and movies to communicate the news "untainted by special pleading or propaganda." He strongly advocated the development of a governmental information service which led to the formation of the United States Information Service, a forerunner of the USIA. Benton, in addition, was instrumental in the establishment of UNESCO, the United Nations Educational, Scientific and Cultural Organization.

Meanwhile, Muzak's research on the effects of music, especially in the workplace, was going full-steam. The Muzak recording studios were engaged full-time in producing training and instructional materials for the armed forces and the Office of War Information. The military was also involved with research on the effect of music in work areas. Functional music by Muzak, their studies asserted, "exercised a positive influence over morale, efficiency and attendance. It has proved a significant factor in the reduction of turnover, the minimization of training and recruitment costs and, most importantly, the escalation of job vigilance." In addition to these studies, the U.S. War Production Board replicated some studies done by the British in the mid-1930's. Increased efficiency, productivity, less turnover, and increased attendance were the findings. *Newsweek* in February, 1942 reported another application of "music by Muzak." In preparation for the air attacks which were believed to be imminent, it was noted that Muzak could stay "on the air" (or "on the line") and provide listeners first with warnings and then with up-to-the minute dispatches from the United Press ticker installed in Muzak headquarters. Radio stations, which could serve as beacons for the enemy bombers, would have long since been off the air. Muzak's leased telephone lines ran underground so to prepare for possible civil defense use, Muzak bought gasoline generators in the event of power failure, secured its midtown Manhattan offices under strong lock and key, and established a wartime studio complete with plywood boards in lieu of windows. *Newsweek* was quick to note that while this practice would be exempt from FCC authority, the dispatches would be subject otherwise to wartime censorship restrictions.

Ever concerned now with programming as an outgrowth of its research, Muzak outlined a specially designed program of air raid music, neither too mournful nor too martial. For its selections, Muzak, U.S.A. drew on the experience of its English affiliate, Wired Redefusion, Ltd. However, no advance publicity was given to subscribers as to which specific tunes would be played, since nervous listeners might panic every time they heard that particular music in conjunction with regular programming.

In January of 1942, Muzak moved from its 17-1/2 hour broadcasting day to a 24-hour basis to facilitate wartime production. It was beginning, in addition, to fine-tune its programming noting the peaks and valleys of worker morale and production. Lunch was a different matter. Since workers had a chance to get together and gripe, Muzak's programming was designed to put shop-talk into the background and, instead, build factory goodwill with medleys featuring employee requests and encouraging sing-a-longs and dances.

By 1946, Muzak was being transmitted to supermarkets, restaurants, offices and factories. Several of these early subscribers have continuously used the service, a period now of forty years: the Big Three auto makers -- Sears, Dow Chemical, GE, and New York's Chemical Bank -- just to give a cross section.

As Muzak prepared for the postwar era, three nagging problems were deserving of the Corporation's time and energies. They were (1) the ongoing row with ASCAP -- the American Society of Composers, Authors, and Publishers, over royalties (2) the development of competition on a local and national level and (3) its fuss with the American Federation of Musicians in general, and James C. Petrillo in particular, over canned music, especially in the lucrative Chicago market.

During the bulk of the war years, a calm had marked the operations of ASCAP since it had come to terms with the

Department of Justice and radio broadcasters in 1941 on the remuneration of its members for tunes broadcast on radio. ASCAP, formed in 1914, was established by publishers, composers, and authors of musical compositions to collect royalties and grant licenses under the copyright laws for the public performance of their works. By 1945, approximately 200 publishers and 1,600 composer/authors belonged to ASCAP giving the organization more than 75 percent control of all copyrighted compositions. Earlier, the inability to reach an accord with the radio broadcasters had elevated such non-copyrighted tunes as Foster's *Jeannie With the Light Brown Hair* to new heights since the radio people were eschewing the entire copyrighted repertoire. The Justice Department intervened finally after a two-year dispute which began in 1939. Now, in early 1945, ASCAP was raising the rates charged not to the broadcasters, but to the small-fry hotels and restaurants. The tactics used were the same as in 1939: raise the rates and step-up checks on compliance. Hoteliers and restaurateurs howled. Compliance was based not on a collection of fees for their use of ASCAP tunes (something that would require constant surveillance), but on such variables as seating capacity, type of entertainment (floor show, dancing, vocalist, etc.) cover charge or minimum, and frequency of performance. For that, the hotels and restaurants would have unrestricted use of ASCAP works. The funds were then passed along by ASCAP to its members.

ASCAP's lead was often followed by the other copyright groups, especially Broadcast Music, Incorporated which was organized by the radio broadcasters in 1940 when they weren't playing ASCAP tunes. Prior to 1940, the only competitor to ASCAP was Muzak's Associated Music Publishers which was eventually sold to BMI in 1947. (BMI was founded by Merritt Tompkins, a former president of Associated Music Publishers, Inc.)

Muzak was not immune to ASCAP's squeeze tactics. While industrial plants were exempted by the copyright groups for the duration (except for the nominal charge of $1 per year), all other users of Muzak now had to obtain ASCAP clearance before using Muzak's product if a copyright infringement suit was to be avoided. (The minimum penalty for copyright infringement was $250 a day.) Muzak had obtained, years earlier, a blanket license from ASCAP whereby it paid ASCAP 10 percent of the gross receipts. But the large sums of money spent to develop the Muzak technique drained the corporation's coffers and Muzak fell behind in its payments. ASCAP finally wrote off a debt of nearly $12,000, but cancelled the contract. Instead, ASCAP turned its attention to the *individual* users and claimed a 95 percent collection rate of Muzak subscribers. Muzak, hard-pressed to sell subscriptions, conveniently failed to inform ASCAP subsequently of its new clients, and when they *did* quote ASCAP rates, underquoted them lest the client fully realize the obvious, i.e., that *two* services were being obtained -- Muzak's and ASCAP's. Reports of the period indicate a doubling of ASCAP's rates and a cutback of Muzak utilization in hotels and restaurants. Eventually, Muzak discerned that their service would be dropped unless ASCAP were allowed to collect at the source and that members of the American Hotel Association would be willing to pay an even *higher* fee for ASCAP material if Muzak would take up the ASCAP license cost. (ASCAP was understandably wary, having been previously burned.) Muzak and ASCAP got together finally and hammered out a deal as reported in *Business Week*, February 9, 1946. Muzak agreed to pay ASCAP a percentage of the gross intake specifically from hotels, restaurants, and businesses, as clearance "at the source" to use ASCAP material.

One problem not faced by Muzak through 1945 was competition. The war helped Muzak retain a kind of monopoly: there was a shortage of equipment, telephone wire and manpower. But there were other reasons. They included the specialized requirements of a sizable transcription library, programming expertise, and plain, old-fashioned financial backing. Muzak still owed its parent, the North American

Company, $4,000,000 in late 1945 -- money borrowed mainly for research. That same year, a spin-off of Decca Records, the World Broadcasting System, became the Muzak's first competitor. Its format and clientele mirrored Muzak's. Initial subscribers included Eastman Kodak, Douglas, and United Aircraft. Distributors were franchised in Rochester, San Francisco, New Orleans, Richmond, and Toronto. Even the vertically cut transcriptions, licensed by Western Electric, were used by World duplicating Muzak. There was one additional commonality: neither company would test the home turf of James C. Petrillo in the large Chicago market, but a report in *Business Week* of August, 1945 indicated that both firms were studying the "Chicago problem."

Muzak responded to its new competition. Harry E. Houghton, an advertising and marketing expert was put in complete charge of Muzak and its associate companies: Associated Music Publishers, Inc. and Associated Program Service, the newest Muzak wrinkle which created and supplied entire musical programs for radio stations. This was a response no doubt to Benton's being involved in so many other projects -- and allowing Muzak to roll along on its own momentum. Houghton demanded and got a bigger advertising budget and a promise to expand geographical markets and services. It was Houghton who personally handled the negotiations with ASCAP to obtain an agreement on royalty collections direct from Muzak rather than individual subscribers.

Early in 1946, Muzak, without formal announcement, entered the Chicago market. It did so by franchising Boom Electric and Amplifier Company, a well-established firm that had installed sound systems in both Comiskey Park and Wrigley Field. Boom also handled Western Electric and Bell Laboratory equipment. Wary of Petrillo, Boom/Muzak promised initially to steer clear of locations that might otherwise employ live musicians, and concentrate instead on offices, retail stores, and industrial plants. Muzak, by coming to Chicago, went toe-to-toe with a local wired-music operator, Marquette Music Company.

Marquette handled Chicago's Walgreen Drugstores, and a number of restaurants and cocktail lounges on Michigan Avenue. Muzak undoubtedly noticed Marquette's streamlined programming concept: one program for industry, one for cocktail lounges and restaurants, and one for offices.

Petrillo, czar of the American Federation of Musicians based in Chicago, was not mollified by the promise of a hands-off policy. By mid-1949, he had threatened to pull the orchestras from all the major hotels in Chicago asserting that the music coming into the lounges and restaurants was not performed by union musicians. *Variety* quotes Petrillo saying that "we have factual reports that in many cities, non-union help or members of other unions do work that should be done by members of the Musicians Union. It has been our rule that where canned music disposes of jobs that could be held by live musicians, we insist that changing of records be done by our members." Boom Electric denied the allegations and claimed their operators were union members, albeit of the Electrical Workers and not the Musicians Union (both of the AF of L.). Petrillo had good cause to be concerned. By July 1949, Muzak's franchise was serving over 300 locations including all the major hotels. Going for the jugular, Boom and Muzak in October of 1949 filed charges that Petrillo and the Union were violating the Taft-Hartley Act. The claim of unfair labor practices against Petrillo was a direct result of his threat earlier to pull the orchestras out of Chicago's leading hotels unless they stopped using Muzak services handled by Local 134 of the AF of L Electrical Workers. In the period between July and October, ten locations had dropped Muzak. Czar or no czar, Muzak clearly had lost its patience with Mr. Petrillo. To add to the pathos of the situation, the electrical workers providing the music were all disabled WW II veterans. Petrillo backed down before the National Labor Relations Board which agreed, in turn, not to file a complaint against the Musicans Union.

It would be the last time that the Muzak Corporation and its local distributors would have union problems of a significant nature; and while that would not be the case for its ongoing dispute with ASCAP and its having to face competition in one form or another, Muzak can be said to have made good progress during the postwar era under Harry Houghton. Its Associated Program Service began creating packaged musical programs for radio stations and also providing commercials, jingles and all, for a variety of commercial lines. All that was required was the insertion of the name of the firm into the appropriate spot in the jingle.

In addition to the music publishing company, the recording studio, the program service, the transmission network, and the research division, Muzak ran a record pressing plant in Elizabethtown, Kentucky. Jimmy Walker, president of Majestic Records and former mayor of New York, asked Muzak to do a private label for his company. Muzak also began pressing the Silvertone label for Sears, as well as other smaller companies. Muzak, with Benton as chairman of the board and Houghton as president, was in its heyday: its product was reaching millions of listeners every day in a variety of situations, in the home, shopping, and while on the job.

All along its research continued. By 1948, the quarter-hour programming, fifteen minutes of music alternating with fifteen minutes of silence, was in place. By 1950, travel Muzak became a reality on trains, planes, and ships. Muzak was now being heard on the land, sea, and air.

A special transcription library was developed in the late 40′s to provide music for Transit Radio -- background music supplied to FM stations broadcasting to public vehicles, i.e., streetcars and buses in the nations′ major metropolitan areas. FM broadcasters and Muzak had determined that this would become an increasingly important field. It *would* become important indeed, but for some very different reasons. The issues raised by the Transit Radio concept would reach all the way to the U.S. Supreme Court and involve claims of audience captivity and violations of the First and Fifth Amendments. As previously noted, the Court′s sanctioning the right of transit radio companies to broadcast to these audiences constitutes the Muzak Society's basis in law. The general programming of Muzak in this period included programs such as "Bunkey the Monkey," the "Ida Bailey Allen Show," and "Beyond Reasonable Doubt." The taped music of the time was performed by a number of respectable artists and personalities: Buddy Clark, Jan Peerce, Rosemary Clooney, Errol Garner, and Mindy Carson. Among the most popular tunes were *Lili Marlene, They're Either Too Young or Too Old, Swinging on a Star, Shoo, Shoo Baby, I'll Be Seeing You, On the Atcheson, Topeka and Santa Fe,* and *It's Been a Long, Long Time,* all favorite standards which were recorded to fit Muzak's specifications.

Billboard on August 13, 1949 reported on the progress of Pacific Network (PN), Muzak's franchise holder in Southern California. One hundred and fifty industrial plants and businesses were paying from $45 to $748 monthly for PN's services. The Muzak segment of PN's services was supplying seventy percent of the franchise's revenue. The future looked bright: subscriptions were up, several new buildings under construction were being wired for Muzak, and cancellations were almost nil. The fact that plant employees and customers were being indoctrinated musically, a circumstance noted in the *Billboard* article, didn't seem to matter. In fact, it was regarded as beneficial to the music business in general "since workers fed daily musical diets become potential record and sheet music customers." PN's operations to eventually include a residential service was deemed "not unlikely." The spokesman for PN reported considerable consumer interest in subscribing to Muzak for home use. Again, cost remained the barrier to such a service with home subscribers paying a hefty $45 per month for the service. Plans were underway at PN to provide residential customers Muzak via radio thereby reducing "costs to a fraction of the present tariff."

Still, the research continued. For five years during the immediate postwar era, Muzak had been conducting a poll among workers. They found that office workers preferred Muzak transcriptions of classical, semi-classical, and waltz music while factory folk liked polkas and Hawaiian music. In all, 50,000 people would be polled with the tabulations broken down by age, sex, regional, educational, and occupational categories. Muzak wasn't running a Top 40 survey, but was instead determining long-term musical tastes to differentiate ultimately its office and factory programming.

One running battle through the 50's had to do with Muzak's relation to services offered by FM stations and its eventual distancing in the public's mind from "easy listening" formats. With the growth and development of FM across the country, Muzak either had to become involved in a significant way with FM broadcasting or have the FCC stop some of the practices of its fledgling competitors. Muzak initially informed FM broadcasters that it would no longer supply programs to FM stations for transit use. One of these, WWDC-FM in Washington was the one involved in the infamous Supreme Court decision discussed in the previous section. Muzak objected to the "commercial use" of its music. WWDC responded by asserting its right to compete with Muzak in the area of functional music and to challenge what WWDC said was Muzak's "beautiful little monolopy." FM indeed was interested in cracking Muzak's hold on subscription music and in some cases went too far. Some FM stations were renting receiving equipment to their subscribers that could eliminate their own commercials, time signals and station breaks. These interruptions would be disturbing, of course, in hotels and eateries, a vast, hotly-contested market. This format was awfully close to Muzak's and so it hired the high-powered firm of Arnold, Fortas, and Porter to stop the practice which they said violated "at least five FCC" regulations. Reports of the period mention FM broadcasts with a "supersonic beep" which eliminated commercials. Successful operations of this type included Marshall Field's Functional Music, Inc., in Chicago and Air Music, Inc., in New York. Muzak in its counter advertising noted the FM's lack of scientific preparation and orchestrations. The FM services were using the "best available music" they said, eschewing costly transcription of the type used by Muzak. Other establishments actually picked up Muzak FM broadcasts and, with the beep device, eliminated the commercials. Cases as late as 1957, when Muzak won a permanent injunction in New Jersey Federal Court against Tel-a-Tune, Inc. have Muzak victorious in every instance. The Tel-a-Tune outfit had installed radio receivers in various commercial establishments that snatched Muzak's signal and with the special device were able to knock out the interruptive time checks and commercials. Muzak cited its twenty-year investment in research and experimentation and won the case handily.

Muzak made it to the White House during Eisenhower's first term and had local franchises owned by such luminaries as Lyndon Baines Johnson in Austin, Dr. Frank Stanton of CBS, the *Philadelphia Bulletin,* Time-Life, Inc., Meredith Publications, and other corporate and business groups. Over 150 franchises were now extant and the Corporation had expanded to overseas operations. Muzak converted to magnetic tapes in the mid-50's opening up the possibility of moving into cities and towns of 50,000 to 200,000 people. Previously, these markets were considered impractical with a disc operation.

In 1957 Benton sold the company to the Wrather Corporation. Muzak's new president was Charles E. Cowley, formerly executive vice president. Cowley retired in 1966 and U. V. "Bing" Muscio became president. Muscio had been executive vice president of the Fedders Corporation. It was "Bing" Muscio who developed what was to be called the "new Muzak."

Muscio created Muzak's "scientific board of advisors" comprised of industrial psychologists and medical professionals who worked with the Corporation's engineers and musicologists. The Board was charged with the creation of a program pattern which would be popular with the customers and at the same time function scientifically in the creation of a musical environment conducive to worker efficiency. The Board's activities led to the creation of a new discipline: the physiological and psychological application of music in social environments. By 1970 Muzak had further developed and refined its sophisticated and highly rational system of programming.

In 1972, the business was sold again. It was purchased to become part of the Teleprompter Corporation owned by entrepreneur Jack Kent Cooke. Cooke who obtained his millions mostly through real estate, counted among his properties the Los Angeles Forum, the Chrysler Building, the Los Angeles Lakers, and the Washington Redskins. Like Victor Kiam of Remington Shaver fame, Cooke was in a Muzak-equipped restaurant when he first heard its product; not liking what he heard, he bought the company. In 1981, Cooke sold the Teleprompter Corporation, which included Muzak, to Westinghouse. In a highly publicized acquisition, Westinghouse forked over $646 million for Teleprompter; Cooke's personal take was $75 million. Westinghouse now became the largest cable and telecommunications company in the world. Muzak was absorbed into the Radio Group W Broadcasting Network.

Muzak continues to refine its delivery system. The early 80's saw the switch from reel-to-reel to cassette tapes and the use of satellites to send its material to franchisers. (There is even an experiment in *foreground music*, called Tones, which is competing against such well-established suppliers as 3M and two other companies, both based in Seattle -- Audio Environments and Yesco. Foreground music is *real* music, albeit "unfamiliar music;" i.e., it is comprised of songs by new artists or non hit tracks from hit albums. *Tones* is aimed at department stores, boutiques, restaurants and other public locations; it consists of a number of 16-hour tape programs which are updated on a monthly basis. Available formats are pop/rock, country, jazz, classical, and several ethnic programs.) Muzak's main business though is still its own transcriptions for background use: simple, familiar melodies arranged with an "almost lunatic lack of expressiveness" as *Newsweek* put it in

1984. Westinghouse's ownership will greatly assist in Muzak's technological development, as now more capital necessary for research and development is readily available.

Chapter 8

FACING THE MUZAK

. . . in the corporate world, the Muzak leaves off where the carpeting begins.

Newsweek

Programming is the secret to Muzak's effectiveness. This programming is created according to some well-defined principles that are the result of considerable scientific research and development dating back to the 1880's. Those basic principles are as follows:

- Music is a successful means of combating boredom.
- Music at work will increase productivity, and in the case of the consumer, keep the consumer in the store longer.
- Music contributes to better employee morale.
- Popular and moderately rhythmic types of music are the most effective.
- Proper scheduling of the music is the most important factor in its effectiveness.

Implementing these principles in a practical sense has been the charge handed to the Muzak programmers since the 1930's. Early on it was thought that the appeal of Muzak rested with the familiarity which it enjoyed in the hearts and minds of those who heard it. In those early years, those who recorded for the company included Harry Horlick and his A&P Gypsies, Xavier Cugat, and bandsman Edwin Franko Goldman. In the 40's, Lawrence Welk and Lester Lanin worked for Muzak, and in the 50's and 60's, Warren Covington, Al Caiola, Mel Davis and Tony Mottola recorded for Muzak. In current practice, Muzak's non-aesthetic arrangements are still recorded by highly competent musicians across the globe; tunes are recorded in a number of different countries: England, Australia, Canada, and

Czechoslovakia -- due to the high cost of recording in the United States.

However, a clearer indication of the musical orientation of Muzak and the value system upon which it rests lies in fully understanding the "stimulus progression" technique. It is this formula for the recording, structuring, and programming of musical sounds that is indicative of the social orientation of the corporation.

Stimulus progression assigns a numerical stimulus value, a stimulus quotient, with a range of 0 to 7 for each composition within its music library based upon the arrangement's tempo, rhythm, instrumentation, and size of the ensemble. By delimitating the range of compositional variables, Muzak can, it believes, assign an objective, fixed numerical value which characterizes the mood or emotional impact the music has upon the listener. The individual arrangements, now accurately rated, can be packaged into whole programs or clusters of selections which can manipulate the psychological moods and thus the productivity or shopping habits of the listener. Muzak's numerous studies have indicated that regardless of the *subjective* reaction to their music, the intent of the experiments to increase output, reduce errors, lower absenteeism, increase sales volume, etc., have all been met. Muzak, to reiterate, works. It didn't always and the refinement of the stimulus progression technique into the powerful tool that it is makes for an interesting tale.

At the time of Muzak's first transmission in New York in March of 1936, the program department consisted of Ben Selvin, director of recording and programming, his secretary, and six full- and part-time assistants, including Donald O'Neill. O'Neill's job was to develop a system that would organize the programs that were created by Selvin. Both were operating under a directive from Waddill Catchings, Muzak president, who had envisioned a system that would create a series of different programs of various lengths that could be coded and stored according to type. In this manner, Muzak would have a library of programs which could be used repeatedly after certain intervals, with the concomitant benefit of reducing production costs. From the master file then, an entire day's programming could be selected and turned over to the studio for transmission.

Well, that was the theory; in practical terms, the system didn't work. It didn't work because Selvin was opposed to repeating a program without making *some* changes. Should subscribers believe Muzak's library to be limited, he felt, would be a problem; straight repetition was an anathema to him. It fell to O'Neill to work out the programming issue. Later, he admitted that in his twenty years with the company, he was never satisfied with the resolution of the repetition issue. Part of the problem was that, especially in the early years, no one at Muzak knew what was needed in the daily program. Muzak was transmitting to restaurants and hotel dining areas with a format that replicated basically those on the radio: hour, half-hour or quarter-hour units of classical, semi-classical, Hawaiian or Gypsy music. Many selections featured vocalists or choruses. Clearly no one had the answer to the programming problem; nearly every Friday, major changes in programming were ordered to be in place by Monday morning. After weeks of experimentation, Catchings sent a memo to Selvin which outlined the format for the programming. This marks the first time, August 1936, that a standardized format would go into place and it would be a precursor to Muzak's current highly effective and top-notch product.

These key points were addressed in the directive: timing, ensemble-size, the use of vocal music, and sequencing. Catchings banned vocals from 9 p.m. to 12:30 a.m. Before 9 p.m., vocals were allowed on that portion of the Red Network that did not assimilate with the premium Purple Network. No tangos or waltzes were allowed after 12:30 at night except when the latter were "hits" and they were used exclusively to start a set, or group of tunes. Selvin and O'Neill were directed to avoid transmitting, as much as possible, slow music. If slow music were somehow unavoidable, it should be placed in the middle or end of a set, *never* at the beginning of a group.

Experimentation continued. Soon it was determined that a pattern which remained constant and which reflected the day-to-day routines of the restaurant was the most effective. The new programming schedule was based on the following pattern:

7:00-9:00	Breakfast Music
9:00-12:00	Background Fill-in
12:00-2:00	Luncheon Music
2:00-5:00	Background Fill-in
5:00-6:00	Cocktail Music
6:00-9:00	Dinner Music
9:00-1:00	Evening Dance Music

Breakfast music was bright and rhythmic, consisting mostly of popular tunes; lunch was a little heavier and featured popular and light-classical music. Novelties dominated the cocktail hour where the emphasis was on piano, vibraphone and Latin tunes. Dinner was similar to lunch and the evening dance music featured name bands with the music getting louder as the evening progressed. This pattern remained with relatively few changes for a number of years. This programming, established for restaurant and hotel eateries, was later to become the basis for Muzak's current program.

Soon it was determined that in the world of functional music, vocals had to be *totally* banned. Singing, unless the performer was live, had no place in restaurants, supper clubs, or hotel dining rooms. Disembodied voices emanating from a speaker in the ceiling was seen by O'Neill and his colleagues to be a nuisance at best, and a distraction at worst. This was extended to all Muzak programs eventually, and, except for a precedent-shattering vocal rendition of "Hands Across America" in Muzak's golden anniversary year of 1986, the ban has stuck.

Of greater importance was O'Neill's discovery of the value of silence. It was not an immediate discovery. Initially, the thinkers at Muzak felt they were selling *music* and not a program. Muzak's initial 17-1/2 hour "broadcast" day was filled solidly with music -- no interruptions, no announcements, no newscasts, no silence. Although trained, mature musicians learn that music is painted on a background of silence, the folks at Muzak had to learn the hard way that *continuous* functional music can be a strain on the ears; subscribers turned it off. It turned out that the working staff, waiters, busboys, hostesses, and cashiers were responsible for the complaints -- not the customers. The programming department inserted a silent interval of up to two minutes every quarter hour to provide a break for those who *had* to listen to the music over long periods of time. Silence meant relief.

O'Neill and his fellow pioneers were gradually developing a set of principles for functional music. Those principles were rooted in psychology, musical perception, and business horse sense. It was already a "given" that no one entered an office, plant, restaurant, or store to listen to Muzak. Ergo, if the primary attention is to be focused on working, dining, or shopping, it follows that the music must avoid elements that distract, interrupt, or interfere with the main reasons people are there in the first place. Music requiring close attention to "be understood" or, at least needing a concentrated effort to be appreciated, cannot be *functional* music. Classical, i.e., art music, in its original form falls into this category, as does avant-garde jazz. Musical elements such as loud dynamics, dramatic shifts in dynamics, non-tonal music or *anything* that startles, surprises, or confuses cannot be allowed; the melody must not only be well-defined (functional music is homophonic music), it must be presented in a simple way: no grandiose, overblown arrangements. A listener's perception of the music, while *not* unwelcome, should merely be a diversion -- the music should at *any* precise moment be listenable, easy to understand, and *easy to follow* so that the perceiver can return "to his main interest" without a sense of frustration or irritation.

Developing "stimulus progression" was the next challenge. Functional music programming differs from the popular concept of background music in that while background music is merely a form of quiet entertainment, Muzak, from the outset, has been concerned with the masking of fatigue and boredom through musical means. It has done so, in an attempt *not* to neglect the basic, inherent entertainment value in the music. To achieve this, functional music in the workplace had to be developed in such a way that a period of increased musical stimulus would offset the normal, hourly fluctuations and downturns in attention. Fatigue and boredom, the enemies of industrial production, had to be combatted; monotony had to be alleviated musically through the skilled use of instrumental timbres, tempo and rhythm variations, and changes in orchestration. Variety, albeit within a limited range, was essential in order to avoid a product so narrow that it would *contribute* to the monotony and boredom it was intended to alleviate, or mask.

Harold Burris-Meyer and Richard Cardinell were the scientists responsible for developing stimulus progression. Both were members of the faculty of the Stevens Institute of Technology in Hoboken, New Jersey and research consultants for Muzak. Their first consideration was to determine the variations in employee fatigue on an hourly basis. They did so in two ways: first, they studied employee output at various points in the day; second, since a predetermined machine speed actually controlled "employee output," they augmented this with a careful inquiry as to what hours in the workday seemed to pass most quickly and most slowly. They plotted the results in chart form and produced what they called the "fatigue curve." Since Muzak served a variety of settings, Burris-Meyer and Cardinell developed a composite curve lumping all the settings either under factories (Figure 1) or offices (Figure 2) based on the characteristics of the workplace surveyed.

Figure 1

FATIGUE CURVE EXPERIENCED BY FACTORY WORKERS AND MUZAK'S PROGRAM STIMULUS DESIGNED TO OFFSET IT

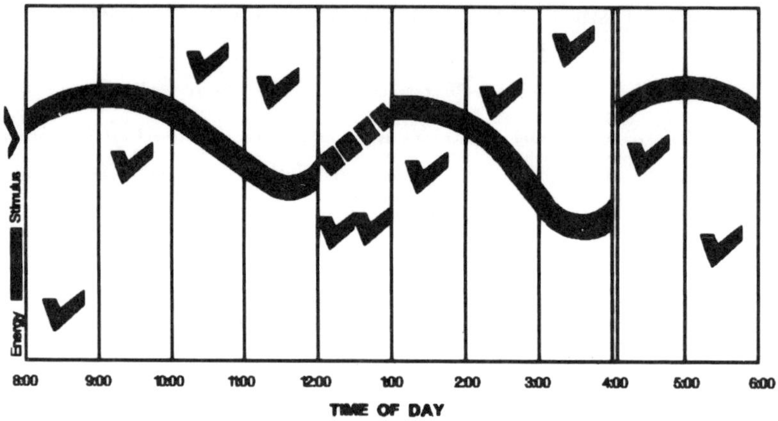

Figure 2

FATIGUE CURVE EXPERIENCED BY OFFICE WORKERS AND MUZAK'S PROGRAM STIMULUS DESIGNED TO OFFSET IT

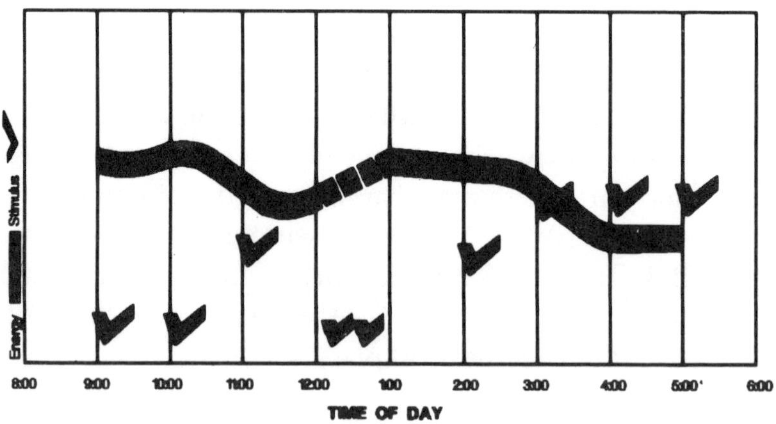

The low points on the curves indicate the hours where worker energy is lowest. These are the times where musical stimulus should be applied.

Studies had shown the investigators that the most effective approach in obtaining stimulation was by using a constant progression of musical "brightness" throughout the group of selections. This brightness can be obtained through the controlling of four musical elements: tempo, instrumentation, orchestration and rhythm. All of these factors contribute to the mood of the selection.

In starting each group, Burris-Meyer and Cardinell recommended the showman's axiom -- having a curtain-raiser of no less than moderate brightness. The succeeding stimulus build-up has a carry-over effect which, they believed, helped determine the spacing between groups and the length of the groups themselves. Burris-Meyer and Cardinell noted that the worker reaches the job in the morning at peak efficiency. There may be some time wasted in settling down to the routine, but, all in all, the best work is done at this time. As time passes, the worker begins to tire: efficiency suffers, production slows, and errors increase. By mid-morning a nadir has been reached. This is followed by a period of increasing efficiency as the lunch hour approaches. The investigators theorized that anticipation of the lunch hour causes this surge. The second half of the day is similar to the first except that a relatively lower point is reached on the scale in the afternoon than in the morning.

To offset the variations in efficiency, Muzak's functional program *mirrors* the efficiency curve. The musical program begins the morning at a low point in stimulation and increases gradually in opposition to the effects of fatigue. The high point of stimulation is between 10 and 11 a.m. Having done its work, the program tapers as the noon hour approaches. The same is done in the afternoon until the end of the work day. The program is not continuous, but, having learned the lessons of the past, is broken into groups of alternate quarter-hours of music and silence. Muzak, in its promotion literature, notes that music can be used successfully up to a total of between 3 1/2 to 4 hours per working day. Beyond that point, it ceases to be effective and, in fact, can be detrimental.

In addition to this rationing of the music, each group of musical selections is assembled on a scale of increasing mood stimulus, or to put it another way, is built on the concept of "internal mood progression." According to the principles of functional music, this provides a feeling of moving forward; it creates momentum to "carry" listeners from the end of one group or set to the next.

Muzak programmers had to deal early on with the problem of reducing the internal stimulus or mood progression of a piece to an objective, quantitative value. The programmers recognized that music, a medium existing intangibly in time and space, has many elements which are open only to intuitive and subjective interpretation and evaluation. They did, however, come upon four elements which they felt could be measured, weighed, and eventually reduced to a numerical value. These were the aforementioned elements of tempo, rhythm, instrumentation, and the size of the orchestra. In a typical, 15-minute segment, the musical selections would vary from about 2 to 3-1/2 minutes in length and there would be approximately 5 to 7 tunes in each group. Muzak uses the following specifications regarding the musical elements:

Tempo. Muzak arranges its music to fall within the standard range of 40 to 130 beats per minute. The first selection in any given 15-minute set may have a beat of 70 pulses per minute. This could then be followed by a piece with 60 beats, followed in turn by a tune with a beat of 90, which would then be followed by one with a beat of 75, then to 100, then to 130, then end with an arrangement of no less than 120 beats. As a whole then, the group shows an average rise in tempo; it need not be steady, however, and the fluctuations are basically random and occur for no apparent reason.

Hypothetically, the group could have begun at 65 beats per minute and then gradually moved up, notch by notch, to 130 pulses per minute. The Muzak programmers learned that this would be a mistake since it would ignore the basic tenet of *diversity* were the music to be *uniformly* progressive in tempo.

Tempo helps establish a regularized pattern of musical movement through time which, in turn, affects the hearer -- both at the physical, muscular level as well as at the mental, psychological one. The role of tempo is therefore critical to creating the perception of movement in an art form that exists only in time. It is ironic that Muzak, so directly connected by the public with mind-numbing blandness is, in reality, very concerned with maintaining an exceptional amount of variation, albeit within stringent limits, lest the danger that the music itself, via the element of tempo, became an added factor in the bringing on of boredom, fatigue, and monotony. Rather than rely on tempo alone, however, and run the risk of boring and monotonous programming, Muzak uses the remaining three elements to achieve the same or similar results, i.e., mood progression. Muzak's promotional literature notes the use of an "ever-changing spectrum of music to develop an increasing mood of brightness essential to functional programming." After handling tempo then as the foremost element in the creation of functional music, the programmers developed principles relating to what they considered the second most critical element: rhythm, or more specifically, meter.

Rhythm. There is a close relationship between tempo and rhythm. Tempo relates to the amount of space between pulses (usually the major pulses) and the maintenance of a consistent rate of speed or movement in time. Rhythm through the metric signs (4/4, 3/4, 6/8, C) and accented beats create temporal movement.

Using the principle that variations in established patterns are not only positive but necessary, Muzak programmers begin an idealized example of a 15-minute segment with a piece in 4/4 time (fox trot, ballad, etc.) then insert a waltz in 3/4 time, another piece in 4/4 time, a samba in 2/2. and conclude with a 4/4 piece. Using Muzak's criteria, there is an overall rise in mood value within this grouping, and, as is the case with tempo, the *pattern* of rhythmic change is uneven. This adds variety and a change of pace.

Instrumentation and Orchestration. Next comes the variable of instrumentation. Muzak once again has a continuum based on its view of the effects of families of musical instruments and their combinations. The strings are at one end of the continuum and are labeled "soft." Next come the woodwinds in the middle and the brasses, finally, at the "forceful" end. Instrumentation coupled with the variable of orchestra size are closely related to the musical element of "timbre," or tone quality or, more precisely, tone color. Timbre is a fascinating musical element that is inextricably connected in music learning with perception, recall, association, and memory. Instrumentation and orchestration play an important role in the recognition and comprehension of music and therefore is of major concern to the programmers at Muzak. They view the strings as producing the most colorful quality of tone, but the most dominating and emotionally exciting are the brasses. The brasses are found alone very rarely in Muzak except for a fanfare. Other than that, in order to operationalize the continuum of instrumentation, subjective ratings are attached to the various instruments and combinations of instruments.

Turning again to a sample 15-minute segment, the programmers deal with instrumentation and orchestration by sometimes eliminating the rhythm section (piano, bass, guitar, and drums) especially if this grouping is present in each tune in a set. If this were the case this important instrument group could not figure in the development of an increasing mood stimulus. Therefore, the programmers delete or add back the rhythm section to develop variety and increase stimulation. The second number in a set, after a moderately lively opener, may *add* strings to soften the sound, eliminate the strings in the third, and return them in the fourth. The set may end with two numbers in a row without strings, just brasses and woodwinds.

This adding and deleting of instrumental families is an important aspect of Muzak programming. They, like composers and music theorists, know that instruments singly and in combination, have different tonal qualities; and tonal quality varies with pitch and loudness. All of this relates to the emotional response thus evoked in a listener.

Closely related is orchestra size. The programmers at Muzak consider this to be one of the most difficult elements to objectify -- not the *number* of instruments involved (that various from a small combo to thirty-two pieces) but the evaluation of how the *ear hears* the difference between say a solo violin, a string quartet, or a full string section. This is a subjective, qualitative judgment, and, in the absence of research literature, Muzak sometimes falls back on the number of instruments used in each orchestral unit.

Muzak can then create over the 15-minute segment, a series of selections based on a simple calculus of musical elements. Using the four factors of tempo, rhythm, instrumentation and orchestra-size, the mood response of a given piece can be determined. For example, a piece may be rated as a "one" in both tempo and orchestration, for a total of two. The rhythm may be regarded as "normal" and has no value assigned to it. Still two. The size of the orchestra, however -- a large one, adds two points, for a grand total of four. Now placed in the Muzak library as a "four," this selection will be pulled when needed to create the mood transition required within any given fifteen-minute segment. The segments then are selected based on the rising and falling of the fatigue curve and their composite stimulus quotient, the stimulus progression curve and fatigue curve mirroring each other.

In a sampler the Muzak Corporation supplies to potential subscribers, the two 15-minute segments consist of *Endless Love, Bette Davis Eyes, The Magnificent Seven, It's a Lovely Day Today,* and *Nine to Five* in the first segment and *Blue Bayou, Hey, Arthur's Theme, Born Free,* and *Le Mauvais Numero* in the second. The selections are presented in "stimulus progressive" order. As for a full day of actual programming, here is the repertoire list as it would be presented in the Public Area Program, i.e., continuous programming:

8:00 A.M.

You Are My Miracle
Mood Indigo
Lonely Cinderella
I'm Easy
Blues for Pussy Galore

8:15 A.M.

A Gentleman in New York
Hawaiian Sunset
I Write the Songs
I'm Leaving It All up to You
I Surrender Dear

8:30 A.M.

We'll Be Together
Without You
Alice's Restaurant
Kiss on My Lips
Macho

8:45 A.M.

The Last Time
Answering Machine
There Oughta Be a Law
I Love You
Movin' Out

9:00 A.M.

Don't Let the Sun Catch You Crying
You Can Never Go Home
Him
Sicilian Sun
She Loves You

9:15 A.M.

Wonder of Wonders
If Dreams Come True
Jessie's Girl
Popsicles and Icicles
Ain't She Sweet

9:30 A.M.

A Step Away
Theme from "La Strata"
Where's the Playground?
Adios
On the Sunny Side of the Street

9:45 A.M.

How's the World This Morning?
The Colors of My Life
Dancing Tambourine
I Do, I Do

10:00 A.M.

Dreams
Colour My World
Sweet Talkin' Woman
All I Ever Need is You
Knock Three Times

10:15 A.M.

Road to Harlem
Please Don't Talk
Chinatown, My Chinatown
Samba Bamba
Jacqueline

10:30 A.M.

Maria
For All We Know
Everybody Knows
Among My Souvenirs
Marina

10:45 A.M.

Tonight
Hold Me
Bill Bailey
I Need a Ray of Sunshine
Grandfather's Birthday

11:00 A.M.

Velvet Moon
Primrose Hill
Sweet Life
After the Rain
Mr. Tambourine Man

11:15 A.M.

Something
Raintree U.S.A.
Who's Gonna Love Me?
Get Happy
What a Difference

11:30 A.M.

Goodtime Chalie's Got the Blues
Annie's Song
Pennsylvania 6-5000
Topaz
East of the Sun

11:45 A.M.

Blue Evening
The Colt
Help!
Blue Velvet
Arthur's Theme

12:00 P.M.

How Are Things
You Made a Dream Come True
Wishin' and Hopin'
Elmer's Tune
Show Me

12:15 P.M.

Peacock Feathers
Did You Ever See a
  Dream Walking?
Island of Lost Souls
Nice To Be with You
Louise

12:30 P.M.

You're a Lady
Looks Like We Made It
Southern Sky
The Last Time I Saw Paris
Theme from "Ice Castles"

12:45 P.M.

Portrait of Tennessee
Love Wise
Chattanooga
Poppyseed Doll
Then I'll Be Happy

1:00 P.M.

Did You Ever Have To
  Say Goodbye?
Don't Turn Me Away
Claudine
My World Is You
Seventy-six Trombones

1:15 P.M.

P.S. I Love You
Steps
We Can Make It Together
Chicago
Tangerine

1:30 P.M.

You Needed Me
You Heard It Here First
In the Mood
I Will Follow Him
You Make Me Feel So
  Good

1:45 P.M.

Over the Hedgerows
Anything Goes
Alley Cat
In the Still of the Night
The Most Beautiful Girl in
  the World

2:00 P.M.

Cherry Pink and Apple Blossom White
A Lovely Way
Shady Lane
Dumbo
Don't Get Around Much Any More

2:15 P.M.

I Miss You So
Time Alone Will Tell
Climb Every Mountain
Travelin' West
Toccata

2:30 P.M.

I Fall in Love
There Must Be a Way
The Laugh's on You
Lover's Sunrise
Little White Lies

2:45 P.M.

The Great Pretender
At Sundown
Do You Ever Think of Me?
Bouncing Bunny
Memories

3:00 P.M.

Call Me Next Time
It Could Happen to You
Someday You'll be Sorry
No Time To Dream
You Should Dream

3:15 P.M.

The Moon
House of the Rising Sun
Because of You
Cat Crawl
Cherish

3:30 P.M.

My Ideal
For Sentimental Reasons
Westward Waltz
I Just Don't Know Why
New York, New York

3:45 P.M.

Young and Warm and Tender
Slow Glide
Manhattan Serenade
Crazy Love
The Look of Love

4:00 P.M.

All by Myself
I'm Not in Love
Sunset Tower
Matchmaker, Matchmaker
Spinning Wheel

4:15 P.M.

Never Be the Same Again
One of These Nights
What Now My Love
Sunbeam
Africa

4:30 P.M.

When You Love
C-Jam Blues
Deed I Do
Dance with Me
Send in the Clowns

4:45 P.M.

Orchids in the Moonlight
Under the Sunshade
On the Way
When Your Lover Has Left
On Green Dolphin Street

5:00 P.M.

Where Is Love?
The Sweetheart Tree
For My Wife
You're Nobody Till Somebody Loves You
Poor Butterfly

5:15 P.M.

Midnight Blue
Tree Top Rockabye
Rock with You
I Love a Rainy Night
Come Back to Me

5:30 P.M.

Love and the World Loves with You
Don't You Believe It
A Cottage for Sale
Should Dreams Come True
Benny and the Jets

5:45 P.M.

Easy
Our Lives Will Touch
American Patrol
I Won't Dance
Honeysuckle Rose

6:00 P.M.

Be Careful, It's My Heart
Deep in My Heart Dear
Girl
Escape
Blower

6:15 P.M.

Hello Dolly
How Much I Feel
Inspiration
Time Is
The Continental

6:30 P.M.

Love Story
A Very Special Love
It's Over Now
I Like Your Style
Stairway to Heaven

6:45 P.M.

One for You, One for Me
For the Love of Him
Happy Wanderer
Bells Ring for You
Moonlight on the Ganges

7:00 P.M.

Easy Come and Easy Go
Crazy She Calls Me
Blue and Brokenhearted
Rosanna
Bermuda Triangle

7:15 P.M.

Life Without You
These Foolish Things
Little Church Around the Corner
I'm a Fool To Want You
Three Little Words

7:30 P.M.

Personally
Tight-Fisted
Dance of the Mayas
Singing in the Rain
Home on the Range

7:45 P.M.

Two Different Worlds
Moon over Miami
That's Love
Mary's Saloon
Rendez-vous

8:00 P.M.

Blue Tango
Midnight Blues Again
Written on the Wind
Anywhere I Wander
Wintertime

8:15 P.M.

My White Knight
Marjorie
There'll Be No Teardrops
New Kid in Town
Voodoo Woman

8:30 P.M.

Colours of Spring
Londonderry Air
A Wonderful Day Like Today
Walk Right Back
I Say a Little Prayer

8:45 P.M.

Shangri-La
The Lady's in Love
Rainy Days and Mondays
Musical Market
Bavarian Dance

9:00 P.M.

Long Before I Knew You
Someday
Double Rainbow
More than Love
Sayin' What I Feel

9:15 P.M.

A Very Special Love
The Soft Life
Let the Good Times Roll
Nobody Wins
Blue Eyes Cryin' in the Rain

9:30 P.M.

Dream a Little Dream
I Don't Know Enough
Can't Help It
Late Love
Let Me Be the One

9:45 P.M.

When I Need You
Who's Crying Now?
Penny Arcade
Downtown
Each and Every Way

10:00 P.M.

I'm Not Myself Today
Torn Between Two Lovers
California Dreamin'
Minor Riff
Tomorrow

10:15 P.M.

Then You Can Tell Me Goodbye
The Edwardians
Breakfast in Ámerica
Honeyuckle Medley
Fine and Dandy

10:30 P.M.

Friendship
Lili Marlene
Always in My Heart
Bubbles
Sweet Surrender

10:45 P.M.

With a Smile
Spectre
Golden Hair
Falling in Love Again
Land of Make Believe

11:00 P.M.

Reality
Girl of My Dreams
Cheatin' on Me
Angel Eyes
This Way That Way

11:15 P.M.

Waltzing Matilda
Do You Believe in Love
Move in a Little Closer
Longefellow Serenade
Tom Thumb

11:30 P.M.

I Wished on the Moon
You're an Old Smooth Talker
I Can't Begin to Tell You
Let the Heartaches Begin
Sambarina

11:45 P.M.

I Like It
More Than Music
My Simple Heart
Lady in Waiting
Swamp Fire

12:00 A.M.

Learning About Love
I Left My Heart in San Francisco
Autumn Dream
The Way We Were
Moonshot

12:15 A.M.

A Nightingale
You're Blase
Singing Waters
Happy Forever
My Way

12:30 A.M.

Nadia's Theme
Village Green
Like Love
Sparkles
Raise Your Glass

12:45 A.M.

They All Laughed
Let It Happen
I'm Getting Sentimental Over You
Odds On
Money, Money, Money

1:00 A.M.

Lilacs in the Rain
Bridge of Signs
Autumn Leaves
Summer of '42
Heart of Glass

1:15 A.M.

Molasses and Honey
Do Nothin' till You Hear from Me
Hang Around
Take Five
Mr. Jolly

1:30 A.M.

Everybody Loves Somebody Sometime
We've Only Just Begun
My Love Song
There's a Small Hotel
I Wish You Love

1:45 A.M.

Time in a Bottle
Sands of Time
Columbus Circle
Dancing Harlequin
Good Day

2:00 A.M.

Beauty
Iris
I Need to Be in Love
Girl from Ipanema
It Could Happen to You

2:15 A.M.

Doin' Right
Where or When
Waltz of the Bubbles
Sunrise, Sunset
What I Did for Love

2:30 A.M.

Classical Gas
Miss You
Meditation
Equinoz
Take the "A" Train

2:45 A.M.

What Do You Want?
My Blue Heaven
Holiday for Strings
Sunset Boulevard
Eleanor Rigby

3:00 A.M.

I'm a Fool To Care about You
Hung on the Wind
Happy Hobo
Be Mine (Tonight)
The Wonderful World

3:15 A.M.

I Love Your Smile
Heartaches by the Number
Song for Cindy
Green Flower
Dancing at the Palace

3:30 A.M.

Would I Love You, Love
Lullaby Song
I Never Know When
Donkey Parade
The Hucklebuck

3:45 A.M.

Spooky
Carolina Moon
Young and Warm and Tender
Tuxedo Junction
Bad, Bad Leroy Brown

4:00 A.M.

It's So Easy Loving You
Only the Lonely
Cast Your Fate to the Wind
Nighttime in Spanish
My Destination

4:15 A.M.

Cotton Jenny
Love Walked In
When My Baby Smiles
Poor Little Rich Girl
Speak Low

4:30 A.M.

I'll String Along
Groovin'
My Baby Just Cares for Me
Make It with You
Midnight in the Oasis

4:45 A.M.

I Can Dream, Can't I?
Flamingo
On the Move
Keep This Train A-Rolling
Tonight

5:00 A.M.

You Go to My Head
Perhaps
Into Each Life
Enchanting Lady
True Grit

5:15 A.M.

Daydream
Boulevard of Broken Hearts
Moonlight Serenade
Embraceable You
Scotch Egg

5:30 A.M.

Now Is the Hour
Bewitch Me
You Needed Me
Upbeat
Devil Eyes

5:45 A.M.

What Kind of Fool Am I?
He Says He Loves Me
Between the Devil
Magpie in Flight
In a Persian Market

6:00 A.M.

The Winner Takes It
Awakening
My Guy
Walk Right Back
One on One

6:15 A.M.

Out of This World
You're the Only Woman
And Now We Love
How High the Moon
Funky Serenade

6:30 A.M.

What Do I Need
Are You Sleeping?
Aquarius
So Near, So Far
You Are Always in My Dreams

6:45 A.M.

Share Your Love
Dance Round the World
Let's Do It
That's Classique
Spicy

7:00 A.M.

Yesterday
Anyway I Say
Coco Chanel
Marigold
Day In, Day Out

7:15 A.M.

Nevertheless
Crystal Belle
Street Car
Music from Across the World
September in the Rockies

7:30 A.M.

Mack the Knife
I Can't Give You Anthing but Love
Two for the Road
Blanket on the Ground

7:45 A.M.

Sing
Believe in Humanity
On the Radio
Somebody Else Is Taking My Place
The Lady's in Love

Muzak's product is created to offset the normal fatigue and stress associated with many of our daily activities. In the workplace, it is a highly sophisticated tool of industrial psychology and labor management which has been created to achieve the objectives of management: quantity, quality, and efficiency as they relate to productivity and profit. For the retailer, it is designed to make buyers out of browsers by causing a physiological reaction reducing stress by lowering blood pressure, pulse rate, and respiration rate.

Muzak's voluminous research record confirms its success in any number of settings. Two of these research projects, from Muzak's own files, will be described here. The first study to be examined was carried out at the United States Steel Corporation's central data-processing center in Pittsburg, Pennsylvania. A total of 81 employees on all three shifts took part in the study. All involved were females, the vast majority of them (83 percent) doing secretarial and clerical work primarily entering data into CRT computer terminals. Most of the women (90 percent) had completed high school, business school, or junior college. It was a young group of workers: nearly half were under 25 years old and 90 percent were younger than forty. In summary then, the subjects were basically a homogeneous group of moderately educated young clerks, all doing the same task of entering data at computer terminals.

The site of the data processing center was a large building occupying a city block. The room containing the center measured 30x100 feet and had acoustical ceiling tiles and other sound absorbers to hold down reverberating noise. No radios were permitted and, until the man from Muzak arrived, there was no music in the center.

U.S. Steel called upon Muzak to reduce monotony, improve the keypuncher's accuracy, and increase their output. Muzak was brought in for six weeks, after which all the subjects received a questionnaire which evaluated the employees attitudes toward Muzak. U.S. Steel also compared the work output of the subjects during two equivalent time periods -- six weeks, where everything was the same except Muzak. Data were gathered for the period just prior to the installation of Muzak and for the six-week period immediately following installation. This comparison considered both the volume of output (total key strokes entered) and accuracy (errors per 1000 strokes).

In the area of employee attitudes, each subject completed a survey describing how she *thought* the music affected her performance and morale. It was in the form of 16 statements with which the subject could either agree or disagree. The employees were almost unanimous (98.8 percent) that they liked the music and wanted to have it continued; only one employee did not. A majority of the employees reported that they worked better with music, that Muzak helped in their work, broke the monotony, counteracted irritating noises, made it easier to concentrate, etc. (See Table 1.)

Table 1

WORKER'S REACTION TO MUZAK

I think Muzak helps me in my work	95.9%
Muzak breaks the monotony of my work	93.9
Muzak helps counteract irritating noises	85.3
Concentration is easier with Muzak	70.4
Muzak helps relieve fatigue	61.8

Similarly, the majority of workers also stated that Muzak made their work-environment more pleasant, made the time go faster, made them feel more relaxed, etc., etc. (See Table 2.)

Table 2

NICER WORKING ENVIRONMENT WITH MUZAK

I like Muzak while I work	98.8%
Muzak makes the time go faster	97.1
Muzak makes me feel more relaxed	87.3
Muzak creates a friendlier atmosphere	84.8
Muzak makes my work more enjoyable	81.4
Muzak gives me a lift	80.7
Muzak makes my fellow employees more pleasant and cheerful	72.9

U.S. Steel compared the workers' efficiency during the two six-week periods, immediately before and after Muzak's installation. At U.S. Steel, keypunch operators are given letter grades ("A through F") for their accuracy. Management found that errors decreased and fewer keypunchers received D's, E's and F's. U.S. Steel predictably decided to make Muzak a permanent fixture in its data processing center. There was one twist in this study. After a follow-up study done some time after the original, it was noted that the volume of keypunching which originally required 108 people, when the baseline data were gathered, later required fewer than seventy workers, about a 50 percent increase in productivity. Muzak, in effect, had cost at least thirty-eight persons their jobs through either layoff or attrition.

The second research study involves a different setting entirely: music in a hospital preoperative holding area. A traditional hospital typically sedates surgical patients while they are still in their rooms before taking them to the operating room. St. Joseph's Hospital in Omaha, Nebraska began using an innovative method in its surgical center to reduce the length of time patients must be anesthetized and thus minimize their stress. At St. Joe's, most patients walk to the surgical center by themselves. Once there, each patient waits in one of many, small private rooms in a holding area until the surgery is about to begin. Patients need not receive any sedation until just prior to proceeding to the operating room.

The chairman of the Department of Surgery (St. Joseph's is affiliated with Creighton University) suggested that Muzak be piped in to these rooms in the holding area to determine whether Muzak could help patients relax while awaiting the knife. Muzak accepted the challenge and installed its system in the holding area. Each of the small rooms had its own volume control. The subjects were a cross section of patients who came to the holding area before a wide range of surgical procedures. There were 286 patients in all, 155 men and 131 women, averaging about 47 years in age.

The patients were divided randomly into two groups: an experimental group that received Muzak, and, on alternate days, a control group that did not hear Muzak. Two nurses evaluated each subject, recording blood pressure, pulse, and respiration rate twice: once when the person first arrived at the holding area, and once again just before the patient left to go to surgery. The nurses also noted behavioral indicators of emotion and evaluated the patient's anxiety levels. A day or two after surgery, each patient rated his or her own anxiety level and described his or her reaction in the holding area.

The experiment continued for several months after which valid and reliable data had been obtained from 184 patients (161 who heard Muzak, and 123 who did not.)

The results are visually depicted in Figure 3.

Figure 3

CHANGES IN PHYSIOLOGICAL MEASURES AFTER WAITING IN HOLDING AREA

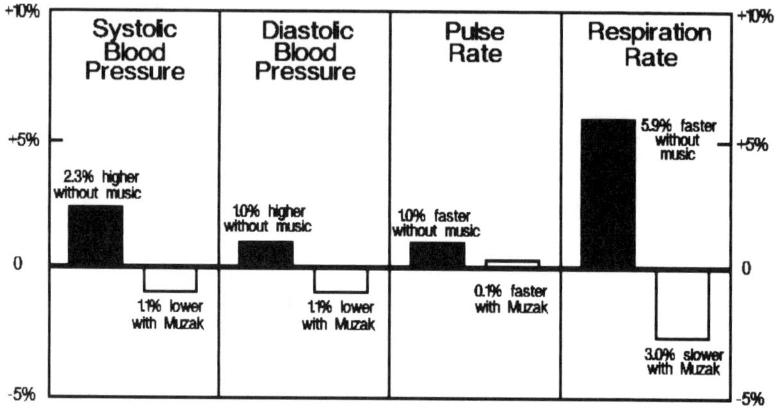

Muzak reduced systolic blood pressure, diastolic blood pressure, pulse rate, and respiration rate. Statistical tests done on the data showed that these charges were very significant (*p* less than .001). The results also demonstrated that when patients heard Muzak, they were less anxious. When the patients heard Muzak, the staff documented lower anxiety levels (statistically significant at the .01 level). The patients themselves who had heard Muzak reported they had felt less anxious. (This finding bordered on statistical significance between the .10 and .05 levels.) When patients heard Muzak while in the holding area, the staff ratings showed they grew calmer; but, without Muzak, the patients became more anxious (statistically significant at the .001 level).

That Muzak is a powerful tool was underscored by the anecdotal reports of the nursing staff. They reported the patients who had heard Muzak were more visibly calm and *resigned,* less worried and depressed. With the Muzak group, the staff noted fewer patients *asking many questions,* trembling, fidgeting and making nervous movements, perspiring and showing startle reactions. The patients who heard Muzak were three times more likely to make positive statements about the holding area at St. Joseph's itself. On the other hand, control subjects who were denied Muzak were about three times as apt to make neutral or negative evaluations about the area. A powerful tool, indeed.

Part IV

THE MUZAK SOCIETY

"In the beginning of human creation, no language such as we now have existed, but only music. Man first expressed his thoughts and feelings by low and high, short and prolonged sounds. The depth of his tone showed his strength and power, and the height of his pitch expressed love and wisdom. Man conveyed his sincerity insincerity, inclinations, disinclinations, pleasure or displeasure by the variety of his musical expressions."

Hazrat Inayat Khan, 1979

Chapter 9

MUZAK THE MENACE

"The right to be let alone is the beginning of all freedom."

Justice William Douglas

This chapter examines the link Muzak provides between today's social structure and consciousness, between patterns of social activity and individual mental processes, and between social reality and individual creativity. It is a discussion of corporate and individual value systems and interweaves both psychological and social processes. Most important, it examines the reason Muzak is a threat to individuality and creativity.

The Muzak Corporation is not unique in its use of technology in the production, packaging, and transmission of music, nor is it alone in the creation of functional music. It is, however, the first, the largest, most sophisticated, and "best," at the use of programmed music. Muzak, in a sense, serves as the best example of how technology has affected music consciousness and individual creativity, and modified, as will be pointed out, the *meaning* of music.

The music that is arranged and transmitted by the Muzak Corporation is Western music, i.e., in the tonal tradition. It is not however, the organization of tones into half-steps and whole steps, or the use of unique orchestration, or the use of it at certain times that makes this tonal product so significant. Rather, the music of Muzak is unique in all of human history in that (1) it was not created by the workers (shoppers or travelers) as they engaged in their activities (2) it is not derived from or related to a specific procedure in these activities, working procedures, or rhythms and (3) the music itself is generally not *about* the workplace, marketplace, or public place. With these observations in hand, we come to the crux of the matter as characterized by the following three questions. If the music heard by individuals in the workplace, marketplace or public place is, in fact, neither created or controlled by them, how does this effect its personally attributed meaning? What do these three unique characteristics of the music of Muzak tell us about our patterns of social interaction and our social structure? Finally, how do we balance or rationalize the manipulative aspects of Muzak with our understanding of individual consciousness, and creativity, especially in a free and open society?

Our final analysis of the Muzak Society begins with the realization that this functional music is imposed upon us irrespective of our actions, desires, or mindset. In the workplace especially, the fact that the music transmitted to the laborforce by the Muzak Corporation is mechanically produced is a critical concept in fathoming its pernicious role in our society. The music heard by the workers, for the first time in history, is now a product of mechanical, technological processes rather than human ones. Until the electric revolution a century ago, music was characteristic of live, socially interactive musicians. The process was one of organizing sounds into a nonverbal system of shared meaning -- the music included not only the sound producers (musicians), but also the audience. Listening and responding to music as well as striking piano keys, plucking, blowing, bowing, hitting, or vocally forming sounds represents a communion of meaningful, purposeful actions. The role of both sets of participants was necessary to the creation of a meaningful social interaction. This interaction has both an internal and shared significance. However, given the ability to record, reproduce, and transmit music, it is only those musicians or technicians producing the recording that are now involved in this symbolic process. Therefore, rather than music being symbolic of a shared social setting, we have music whose significance is derived from a series of social activities (the recording sessions) that have occurred prior to the music actually being heard by the listener. Recorded music does not include the listener in an active communication process, it merely recreates past action and, in fact, tends to *exclude* the listener. Sensitive music lovers know this. Why otherwise go through the many hassles of "seeing" a live performance (rock, pop, musical, opera, symphony) when records and tapes of the music are readily available? It is, of course, the interaction involved, the shared meaning of the rituals and conventions engaged in by performers and audience alike that make these events more vivid in the human imagination than their prepackaged counterparts. There is a fundamental point here if one is to fully understand the change in what we are trying to convey in the phrase, "the *meaning* of music." Prior to the development of a means to record and electrically transmit sound, music was deeply symbolic: it was a social symbol unique in its non material and transitory form whose meanings were derived, by necessity, from immediate, shared, real, situational activity. The music, requiring the presence of both live and active musicians and an audience, contained personal and social meanings that intimately related to the actions engaged in while the music was being created. Music was connected directly with planting crops, eating food, praying to God, and marching to war; music was meaningful because of its link between the immediacy of it own creation and the individual consciousness of persons involved in social activity. In the most natural of settings, music was a mediator by tying action to symbol and giving form to movement via the proper patterning of sounds. Music, therefore, has multi-level qualities not the least of which are those related to social activity and interaction. The transformation of this shared but personally created symbolic system by the introduction of a new technology goes beyond a change in the acoustical qualities of musical sounds; it has implications for our view of modern day, post-electric revolution social interaction. Certainly this is not the first time an observer has considered the dynamics or implications of this change, but it is important to have reviewed it in the context of the Muzak Society, for it is one of its building blocks.

This takes us to the second characteristic of functional music, i.e., its unrelatedness to any specific procedure, work, purchasing process, or rhythm of the workplace, marketplace, or public space.

The functional music of the Muzak Corporation is not derived from any specific work, leisure, or shopping practice. It is designed to be unobtrusive in all of these settings, and, in the case of Muzak in the workplace, it is related to the universal and standardized conceptions of labor practices developed to facilitate industrial production. These work practices may be specialized in their particular motions, but these movements are interchangeable from one workplace to another, e.g., a typist can be an active member of *any* typing pool, an accountant can be used in *any* accounting department. Since today's industrial practices are departmentalized and strictly delineated, it stands to reason that the music introduced into this setting would be a highly rationalized tonal system in sync with other industrial labor practices. It is this concept of interchangeability that characterizes Muzak's view of time and space: this mechanically transmitted music typifies the cultural concept of time not varying; time is managed in the same way for all workers, at all work sites. The work practices all follow one time, one tempo, one rhythm. This is a model which is concerned with efficiency and productivity, where the pace can never falter over an eight-hour shift. It is to these *ends* that Muzak's functional music is formulated.

As previously noted, to achieve efficiency and enhance productivity, the programming department at Muzak creates, programs, and transmits during one working day ninety-six quarter hours of music following the dictates of the stimulus progression theory. Recall too that the worker will hear then approximately sixteen of these segments what, with Muzak's interspersing 15-minute blocks of silence between sets. A worker hears one-third of the approximately 480 tunes played each day, and, according to this highly rationalized formula, work begins at a high energy level regardless of the actual starting time. We have seen from Muzak's studies that this high energy level gradually deteriorates as the work period progresses except for a small upswing near the midpoint and quitting time. Muzak's stimulus progression technique, of course, is programmed to fight the tapering off of energy and the subsequent decrease in productivity: it begins with low stimulus music and ends with high. Initially, common logic would tell us that increasing the tempo of the selections would control this tailing off of efficiency. And, of course it does, to some extent. Classical conditioning experiments for many years have shown that music affects heart rate, respiration, and muscle tension, and therefore, properly programmed, music could counter worker inefficiency as the day progresses. Succinctly, music creates a response which alters natural body rhythms and work habits.

This is ground that we've already covered, of course, but this ability to physically affect worker activity bears repeating; it is, however, only one aspect of functional music's significance. For its additional significance we turn to the music's programming as it relates to our concept of consciousness and time. Muzak's fifteen minutes on and fifteen minutes off strives not only to obtain a physiological response, but to repackage our cultural orientation towards the passage of time. Muzak attempts to *control* time. It does so by programming a highly rational, ordered sound world. Sound moving over time, as in music, can be adjusted in the sound environment and thereby monitor the individual's perception of the movement of time. Consider how it works: the continual reappearance of the music, its carefully regulated on and off, just below conscious apprehension, assures that the listener will be always aware of the motion and smooth passage of time. Voila! There are now external indicators as to how the day is progressing. During the 10:30 a.m. slump, the music is upbeat, sassy, brassy; it will be subdued just following lunch only to become more stimulating as the day begins to drag. But, maddeningly, we *know* that it will be there -- always, regardless of the specifics of the hour, the day of the month, our blurred vision or aching feet.

The regular and exact timing of Muzak's functional music offsets the chance of innovative elements from interfering with steady productivity. As the work has been regulated to be more efficient and individual, idiosyncratic methods and routines openly discouraged, functional music as it is used in the workplace virtually eliminates individual, idiosyncratic or chance musical occurrences from developing. The richness of an entire heritage of work music which emanated from the workers and was drawn upon their experiences is non existent. This functional music should not be compared to the field-holler, the serene music of the quilting bee, or any of the emotional and heartfelt verse which characterized the feelings, attitudes, and sensitivities of pre industrial labor. This music of the industrial age is handled in the same way as the machinery: smooth, steady, and well-oiled. The fantastic image borne from the movie *Metropolis* of humming wires, electro-magnets, dials, and levers producing the forever steady sine wave is not unlike the normal curve configuration of functional music as it drifts in and out of the victims' consciousness in fifteen-minute cycles.

In marketing a tonal product for use interchangeably in any setting, the meaning of the music is once again removed from the moment of its creation. Workers don't create Muzak in the office, shoppers don't create functional music in the supermarket. The music doesn't reflect any actual happenstance in the workplace (*Just Whistle While You Work*?) It's just there, not reflecting any particular social activity, but just activity in general. But music is not created in a vacuum; it has to have some social context. We know that Muzak generally arranges music heard first on radio, television, and motion pictures; these arrangements are popular and familiar musical standards. The arrangements are purely instrumental, containing no lyrics. This familiarity on the one hand and the removal of lyrics on the other provides us with a clue to the Inner Muzak -- a clue that takes us back to a consideration of music as a symbol and that enigmatic process we call creativity. With that, we come upon an even more exotic psychological consideration: memory, recall, fantasy, and personal wish fulfillment.

There are a number of studies providing evidence that the lyrics and melodies of familiar tunes hold an inner message that is usually hidden from conscious thought. This inner message reflects not only the person's mindset but, if you'll allow, his or her heartset. As evidence of these haunting melodies or lyrics, we note those people who unconsciously hum or sing a tune; this is the voice of the preconscious and can be understood in the same manner as the fragment of a dream or a fantasy. These minor musical excursions hold a symbolic meaning for the person taking them. Likewise, previous social interactions or settings can be recalled by individuals hearing a familiar tune on the radio or tape player. These responses can be just as strong as those developing out of personal memory. On a large scale, this explains the cyclic reappearance of nostalgic, musical revivals: Big Bands, beach music of the early 60's, etc. Furthermore, it is clear that this recall of a melody, or even a fragment, can evoke an emotional response in the present unrelated to what's happening at that specific moment. Music has the power to evoke psychic states removed from rational waking consciousness; this is both the challenge facing functional music programmers and the menace they pose when successful as in Muzak.

The absence of lyrics in Muzak is an interesting issue, especially considering that their removal is to ensure that Muzak remains "felt" and not heard. By using popular and familiar reconstituted music that is melodically familiar, no one can measure the extent to which the lyrics may emerge from the memory banks of the listener. This explains the success of Muzak in the workplace by evoking mental states removed from the actual work process and the workers themelves. This capacity to evoke emotional states of preconsciousness removed from the laboring process rests on the use of popular and familiar music. A balancing act is taking place: the music cannot distract through lyrics, volume, instrumentation, or rhythm, but through the use of familiar melodies, the music retains the capacity to subliminally remove the listener to another emotional state.

Before leaving the missing lyrics issue, there is one further consideration. The lyrics missing from Muzak are predominately about love and friendship. This is because Muzak reformulates top 40 pop tunes, most of which deal with one or more of the five operational stages of a relationships: "prologue" (thinking or fantasizing), "courtship" (active search or wooing), "honeymoon" (happy stage), "downward" (breakup), and all alone (isolation). That brings us to the role of fantasy as it relates to functional music and Muzak's product. Fantasy is private knowledge that cannot be removed from sensory properties; in fantasies, the mind and body are linked for they are dualistic in nature -- using symbols which mediate between mind and body. In fantasies, too, through the use of symbols, we are permitted to think, act, and feel far beyond the verbal meaning one attaches to the world. What does this have to do with functional music? Well, in the perception or apprehension of music, the listener reacts and feels the musical sensations far beyond the rationally conscious capacity to give them verbal meaning. All sounds are sensed, regardless of the meaning or lack of it attached to the sensation. Music as a form of thought and knowing, and fantasy as a form of thought and knowing gives meaning to these perceptions, emotions, and sensations. With Muzak, especially in the contemporary work setting, the rhythm, tempo, harmony and melody are designed to give form to these preconscious sensations, emotions, and perceptions.

Let's explore the relationship between fantasy and music further. A fantasy or daydream is an ordinary mental phenomenon, and, just as we all dream, all of us have fantasies. (Note the distinction between dreams and fantasies. A dream is a complex mental process markedly different from a fantasy in that it is not in the form of rational working thought processes.

Dreams can be hallucinatory; they are often illogical, emotionally powerful, highly condensed and distort logical time-oriented structure. Because of the latter, dreams do not figure in this discussion as they are not constrained by time and space as fantasies are.) Fantasies occur when we are awake as distinguished from dreams. In a fantasy, the individual remains in touch relatively with the external reality, more so than the dreamer; in the former, bodily senses are more in tune with the external physical world and there can thus be more interplay between the external and internal. Fantasies are a type of nonverbal, visual imagery which emerge from the wishes and desires of an individual; fantasies relate our inner and outer worlds in a very special way and are usually *fulfilled* within the limits of the fantasy.

Fantasies are projections, a person's way out of the current moment, while still being conscious of that moment. Fantasies are not simple, linear thought patterns, but representations of wishes and desires portrayed as complete images created by the individual's beliefs, values, and judgments. These beliefs, values, and judgments link an event or occurrence in the present to memories established from past actions; once tapped, these associations wind their way back and forth between the dimensions of past, present and future fantasized actions. Fantasies are rehearsals and, in part, wish fullfillment; they are residues of the psyche based on previous experiences which have become attached to more recent and immediate events in such a manner that they allow an individual to envision a future or past idealized state.

Music has a number of features which evoke mental states similar to those in fantasies. Music creates within an individual a mental state on a continuum between the strictly logical and rational and the highly emotive, sensory mental state. The mind can process musical stimuli nonverbally, i.e., without resorting to mere words and formal language structure. Music, as a non material entity must be relived and/or recreated each time it is to be apprehended. Likewise, a fantasy is a fantasy at the moment of its conception; given another form, say in language, it then becomes something altogether different: a poem, short story, or novel. Music and fantasy have meaning insofar as they are attached to the immediate, internal, physical, and emotional sensation perceived at a unique moment. Their power, likewise, rests in their being subjective, hidden and emotional mental states. Music is related to fantasy in its capacity to refocus conscious attention from external reality. Music and fantasy involve mental processes that create an inner reality fitting the internal beliefs, values, and dynamics of the individual. Non-Muzak music, which might be live or, more likely, traditionally produced, may help structure the activities in the workplace, or perhaps divert attention from the repetitiveness of the tasks at hand. This diversion, however, is directly connected to the music-making itself with little if any overt alteration of the worker's time and space. In Muzak, the music acts unconsciously to redirect the worker's sense of reality; "real" time and space are altered in the worker's consciousness.

This alteration of time and space takes one of two forms, *retrospective fantasy* or *projective fantasy*. Both are basically self-explanatory. Retrospective fantasies are historical images and memories involving reminiscence or nostalgia; projective fantasies involve wish fulfillment and rehearsal set in a future time and place. Both mental states are internal alterations of consciousness and result in the individual's no longer being fully attentive to external reality.

In considering retrospective fantasies, it is important to distinguish between reminiscence and nostalgia. Nostalgia is defined as "the state of being homesick," or the "yearning for the return to or of some past period or unrecoverable condition." It is a regressive state, and, in its more virulent form, is considered a form of depression. Nostalgia, with its acute longing, idealization of the past, and realization that the loved person or object is gone forever, is a common theme in music. One example of this is *Yesterday* by Lennon and McCartney:

Yesterday, all my troubles seemed so far away

Now it looks as though they're here to stay
Oh I believe in yesterday.
Why she had to go I don't know, she wouldn't say.
I said something wrong now I long for yesterday.
Yesterday, love was such an easy game to play,
Now I need a place to hide away
Oh I believe in yesterday.

In reminiscence, as contrasted to nostalgia, the mood may be neutral, bittersweet, or even joyful, as the individual wallows in the feeling that the past has not been lost forever, but is still available. In reminiscence, one need not yearn hopelessly, since the loved one or object can be recalled, examined, and contemplated in the mind. There is undoubtedly pleasure and satisfaction derived from this exercise of one's memory; here, the gratification comes not only from the recollections themselves, but also from the *process* of remembering. Johnny Mandel's *The Shadow of Your Smile* and countless thousands of songs embrace this theme. In Muzak, only the melody is present, of course, but the hidden memory of the lyrics create an emotional affect unrelated to the present.

The shadow of your smile, when you are gone
Will color all my dreams and light the dawn.
Look into my eyes my love and see, all the lovely things you are to me.
Our wistful little star was far too high
A shadow kissed your lips and so did I.
Now when I remember spring, and all the joy that love can bring,
I will be remembering, the shadow of your smile.

Another example is the theme from *Love Story*:

Where do I begin to tell the story of how great

a love can be,
The sweet love story that is older than the sea,
The simple truth about the love she brings to me? Where do I start?
With her first hello she gave a meaning to this empty world of mine;
There'd never be another love, another time;
She came into my life and made the living fine.
She fills my heart with very special things,
with angel songs, with wild imaginings.
She fills my soul with so much love that anywhere I go I'm never lonely.
With her along, who could be lonely?
I reach for her hand, it's always there.
How long does it last? Can love be measured by the hours in a day?
I have no answers now, but this much I can say:
I know I'll need her till the stars all burn away and she'll be there.

Reminiscence is important to mental health; it plays an important role in the development and maintenance of one's identity. Reminiscence is personal roots. It is one way an individual relates to the old but, nevertheless, vital parts of the inner self. An individual's sense of self is anchored by a set of discrete events and happenings whose availability to the mind's eye provides stability, and, over time, self-identity. In a work or social setting that is monotonous, dead end, tedious, anxiety-producing or frustrating, the music can provide a necessary release-valve to maintain self-identity and mental stability.

Reminiscence has one other function. It provides a safe outlet for erotic and aggressive impulses and serves future-oriented goals by permitting an appropriate review of both past accomplishments and failures. In this function, reminiscence comes close to projective fantasy as it creates a mental state that is in the form of a rehearsal or trial action. Reminiscence brings the past back to life in the mind as enduring representatives to be re-experienced; here, the past and present merge.

Projective fantasies are also linked to the past and give form to mental images created by present-time hopes, desires, and wishes. This is exemplified by the song, *Someday My Prince Will Come*:

Someday my prince will come,
Someday I'll find my love,
And how thrilling that moment will be,
When the prince of my dreams comes to me.
He'll whisper, "I love you,"
And steal a kiss or two,
Though he's far away,
I'll find my love someday,
Someday when my dreams come true.

The projective fantasy is in a future time, an image of self unfettered by past failures or current expectations, yet formed by them. The reality of the listener is projected to another emotional time and place. It can almost be escapist as in Jim Webb's *Up, Up and Away*:

Would you like to ride in my beautiful balloon?
Would you like to glide in my beautiful balloon?
We could float among the starts together, you and I,
For we can fly! We can fly!
Up, up and away, my beautiful, my beautiful balloon!
The world's a nicer place in my beautiful balloon.
It wears a nicer face in my beautiful balloon.
We can sing a song, and sail along the silver sky,
For we can fly! We can fly!
Up, up and away, my beautiful, my beautiful balloon!
Suspended under a twilight canopy
We'll search the clouds for a star to guide us.
If by some chance you find yourself loving me,
We'll find a cloud to hide us, keep the moon beside us.
Love is waiting there in my beautiful balloon,
Way up in the air in my beautiful balloon.
If you'll hold my hand, we'll chase your dream across the sky,

For we can fly! We can fly!
Up, up and away, my beautiful, my beautiful balloon!

Our images of the future are closely linked to daydreams and fantasies. Associated events from the past sparking projections of the future continually invade our consciousness and become integrated with our patterns of action and meaning. In Muzak, what has been created through a scientific, systematic, and highly rationalized process, is the ritual alteration of time and space. In a fashion, this is no different than the occult rituals of nonliterate cultures, where the spirits of the past are transported to the present in order to change current circumstances. However, the difference in the case of Muzak is that this contemporary ritual is employed in a manner disallowing human interaction. Muzak, transmogrified from popular music, organizes, at the conscious and unconscious levels, mental processes related to the perception of reality. Muzak is a highly sophisticated, technologically advanced form of social control, the manifest control of the aural environment, the latent control of symbolic action.

For some time now, the industrial labor process has been characterized by the need for discipline. This cultural imperative, after a century of dealing with industrial labor practices, dictates that the work force be tightly scheduled, structured, and controlled so that the necessary ends be met. The modern workplace relies both on the capacity of the individual to be self-disciplined as well as external means which are designed to increase efficiency and productivity. Muzak, of course, is one of these external means. The requirements of this managing personnel in the workplace necessitate the repression of a number of forms of activity considered a hindrance to performance: talking, leaving the work station, leisurely coffee drinking, gossiping, etc. The modern worker cannot succumb willy-nilly to any emotional or physiological desire, wish or impulse on the factory line, in the typing pool, as a cashier, or at the word processor. Here, Muzak, imposed on the work force, plays its effective role. Music, as a sensory stimulus, whose meaning is symbolically integrated by the worker's consciousness via prior experiences, transforms the repressed psychic energy of the worker into socially acceptable internal images that are controllable within the discipline of the work setting; the images are those related to the meanings suggested by the missing lyrics in the music. The Muzak Society is thus one of controlled consciousness and is hierarchical: the Muzak leaves off where the carpeting begins. The Muzak Society is one of strict management authority, of externally imposed ends, of regulated, repressed emotions. The Muzak Society is subtle social control having a benign socio-historical context; it is a perverse reformulation of a highly valued type of social interaction whose meaning has been masked behind the experience of hearing music while engaged in work.

The control does not come from only the musical tones themselves, but also from the careful monitoring of the silence that surrounds the music. Silence itself is a powerful symbolic form. In western culture, silence is an important indicator of the beginning or end of an expression. In western music, the use of silence is delberate by the composer or conductor in order to emphasize the commencing or ending of a musical expression. Consider the composer's use of the Grand Pause and the charged silence before the last "Hallelujah" in Handel's "Hallelujah Chorus" from *Messiah*; consider the conductor, baton poised ready to begin the next symphonic movement -- he controls the aural space by controlling the pause, the rest, the silence before and after the music. This space, however, is a void; it lacks vitality, and, symbolically, life. The music finally beginning brings energy, vitality, and change that are the essentials human of existence.

Individuals subjected to Muzak are symbolically controlled by its silence. Heretofore, where previous uses of pausing, resting, and silence were controlled by the workers, this mechanical music appears, disappears, and reappears at the edge of consciousness; the reappearance coincides with the workers' starting to become bored, fatigued, and anxious. In the endless continuity and repetition of the modern workplace, the fifteen-minutes-of-silence segment allows for a necessary respite, at the same time that it constantly reassures the listener of movement.

Thus Muzak, except in the Public Area format, is not perceived as one continuous tinkling in the background, but is broken into discreet segments of time. Here, the time is measured by a universal and rational pacesetter. Within each unit is a song title capable of eliciting reminiscence or projective fantasies, facilitating the alteration of the subjective perceptions of time.

Time in the workplace moves in a linear fashion between yesterday's work and tomorrow's work, between past events and future plans. Time moves and yet there is no individual creation of *closure* in time. Muzak *creates* that sense of closure, an illusory sensation of movement in time and space within a highly structured and rationalized structure. With Muzak, there *are* apparent beginnings and endings in the fifteen-minute sets, yet, in reality, the live, interacting human being is far removed. Muzak affects the most hidden and powerful aspects of an individual's psyche: daydreams, fantasies and hidden emotions. It alienates the worker from the creative process and personal, individual meaningful creation. Sensitive, perceptive individuals rebel when subjected to Muzak because they somehow perceive, on whatever mental plane, its robbing effect. Muzak is not music as such, but instead is the distant, abstract voice of authority and control.

Chapter 10

Is it Live or is it Memorex?

"Until about fifty years ago, it was believed that music was always composed to be involving, to capture and hold your attention. We discovered that when properly arranged and recorded, music could be used to do just the opposite."

Muzak Blurb

It now can be reasonably asserted that by the mechanical reproduction of music, the definition of this art form was fundamentally changed. Where once only humans could make music or play music, one now *plays* a tape which makes the music. Musical knowing, or knowledge about music-making also is changed: music need not be "known" to be created. What is of more importance is the knowledge of the machine. Music as a meaningful process of artistic interaction between people or as a product of one's own imagination or creation is not germane to contemporary considerations of the art. This is not mere replacement of one method of musical production for another. It is rather the conscious, rational replacement of human interaction with a mechanical pseudo-interaction. The ability to create an aura of interaction where none exists, to establish the feeling of shared meaning where none exists is a powerful cultural illusion. There is irony here. Historically, music was symbolic of the *gestalten,* the whole; it gave meaning and credence to shared action; it gave emotional expression to social interaction in rituals. Music, in its new role as an object, is now a commodity; it is a product like any other not valued any longer for its aesthetic meaning but, instead, for its ability to garner capital and increase profit. What is required now to hear or make music is not other people, but the down payment to purchase a home entertainment system: turntable, tape player, and speakers; the TV and VCR to preserve MTV is an added bonus.

In the Western world, there always has been a musical performance tradition, especially in the music of the elite, i.e., high art, involving an active performer and a passive audience. Isn't the condition noted above just a technological extension of this gulf? Hasn't the human as performer just simply been replaced with a machine as the performer? It is obvious that the two are seen as interchangeable. Otherwise the "Is it live or is it Memorex?" question wouldn't be such an effective advertising slogan. At its basis is the assumption that while the performer is implied but not present, the meaning of the music is not affected. Moreover, the technology to record, store, and retrieve sound, and the development of a rational, successful functional music for all settings has assisted in maintaining a culturally specific form of social interaction. It is a form of social interaction, i.e., musical performance, that promotes, stresses, and preserves the gulf between performer and audience. Since the meaning of music appears not to have been altered in the public's eye, then we are left with a further by-product of the Muzak Society: the further distancing of the wide gulf between performer and audience.

The language of the Muzak Society is becoming a universal language, what with its transmission throughout the world. Received in twenty-five countries, Muzak collides with an indigenous music culture that in many cases still preserves the critical link between performer and audience. In many of these cultures there remains a vital form of social interaction, musical performance, which meaningfully unites performer and audience in a shared experience. Muzak's effect on these societies, as the quintessential musical product of western technology, will be interesting to watch. Given the power inherent in the new sound technology, the power to dominate acoustic space, the matter becomes a question of cultural imperialism. One can only reflect on the cultural repercussions that this introduction of a seemingly benign technique will have on societies when they begin to receive their uplinked, downlinked, satellite-boosted, universal functional music.

Modern technology is more than mere improvement in the tools of a society; it can be a way of organizing the world. Now, most of that which is within human reach can be rebuilt, reconstructed, and reincorporated into this new system of technical rationality, including social relations. Traditional social structures and systems of social interaction are altered by this pervasive, over-riding technical rationality.

Again, Muzak is not the only organization to use modern technology to the fullest in the production and dissemination of music; however, Muzak is unique in its being consciously created and tested along scientific principles. The Muzak Corporation characterizes very well the scientific method which dictates that the investigators separate, analyze, and categorize phenomena in order to better understand, predict, and control them. The fundamental *meaning* of this functional, highly rationalized music is social control. Muzak, always sparkling in the background, is a nonverbal symbol of scientific triumph and authority, of technological power designed ultimately to maintain the present social order.

In order to survive, societies need to change over time in any number of ways including the redefinition of the social order. During periods of technological breakthroughs and social change, the social structures and institutions emerging from this reorganization are quickly perceived as "normal," or "that's the way it is." They quickly become the accepted social order and take on a life of their own. The viability of these new structures is tenuous however, and they really cannot tolerate opposition, defectiveness, idiosyncrasy, or dysfunction. In fact, the characteristics of opposition and sub-par performances are typically perceived as a threat to the social order, an anathema to the smooth running, i.e., survivability, of the system. In the past, protection against dysfunction was often met with force as exemplified by the breakdown in labor-management relations with strikes, lockouts, slowdowns, and job actions. A far more subtle response to perceived dysfunction by management involves no overt force at all. Instead, sources of opposition and dysfunction are isolated, examined, neutralized and then transformed and reincorporated as functional parts of the natural order. Muzak, by providing management with music for the workers, has isolated, examined, and transformed those aspects of the work process deemed dysfunctional, e.g., the slump of productivity in mid-morning, the unnecessary chatter among workers, and the high rates of absenteeism. This functional music, as used in the workplace particularly, serves to reinforce the existing social order. Those romantics who compare it to the work songs of miners, cowboys, sailors, and field hands couldn't be further off base. These songs were produced *by the workers* and often were critical of their plight, allowing them to express their dissatisfaction without fear of penalty. Mechanically produced functional work music, on the other hand, is a subtle mode of social control. In Muzak, it is a means whereby the internal psychic states and mental processes of the workers can be discreetly redirected. Muzak affects these mental processes by which retrospective and projective fantasies and daydreams are created, calling upon nostalgia and reminiscence to redefine the worker's reality.

It is not enough to say that Muzak is a highly subtle and sophisticated form of social control; it goes beyond that. It is the ultimate example of how traditional meanings and social processes can be altered by technology. Here we are reminded of Herbert Marcuse's analysis of the one-dimensional man. He asserts that in the course of modern history, human beings have produced a social system, a language, and a way of knowing that permits no lasting opposition. Gone are the dialectical forces of opposition and radicalism that are the primary ingredients of creativity and imagination; they have been buried by the unrelenting, single-minded juggernaut that is the modern technological society. What's left is the repetitive reaffirmation that technology will find for us those efficient and productive solutions to our existence; it is a superficially pleasant world.

And Muzak is right there with its description of its commodity: the sound that says "everything's going to be all right." The vital, dynamic, multidimensional structures of previous history, which included the active social processes that produced music, have been replaced by one-dimensional structures designed for functional and efficient ends. It is this climate that fosters Muzak. This music is not the voice of the work effort, but the sound of control over labor, the sound of order and authority.

Consider again the subtlety of it all. The viability of this order and authority rests with its initial acceptance within each individual's psyche and its subsequent reaffirmation through repetition. The control of individuals in the workplace is so thorough and pervasive that there is no need for coercion to bring it about. Worker acceptance of the regulations of the workplace is implicit in the very structure, content and form of this music as it is imposed on the workers; after all, this is functional music. It parallels the desired ends of industrialized society: efficiency, productivity, and profit. The reality of this overt, preconscious control, seemingly impossible, Orwellian, or absurd in earlier settings, is now "normal" and an accepted, integral part of our lives.

Muzak was developed following the accepted principles of social science and economics and promoted by entrepreneurs to maintain high production and efficiency levels. Muzak has transformed the workplace, the supermarket, department stores, and even the Oval Office by changing the aural evironment. It has also altered a fundamental assumption of what music is. No longer intrinsic to social interaction and a symbolic mode of meaningful, nonverbal communication, music, as treated by Muzak, is an object. As an object, music acquires a status free of any specific social setting, and, as an object, can be exchanged or sold. Music, in the hands of Muzak becomes a perversion: a commodity whose value is measured by its ability to promote efficiency and productivity. Music, as a commodity, is imposed on people by Muzak in a variety of situations and, clearly, it affects individuals, but is not, in turn, affected by these individuals.

Muzak is not the music of people. People engaged in the labor process or other activity exposed to Muzak do indeed experience an emotional reality separate from the reality of the task or moment at hand. Its effectiveness grudgingly conceded, we must remember that Muzak is not symbolic of human interaction and involvement, but of human separation, isolation, and exclusion. Sadly, not only is the individual separated from the rest of humanity in the production of a wonderfully expressive symbol, but he or she is removed from the reality of his or her own emotional response to this art as they go about their activities.

"By creating a fuss about sounds, we snap . . . back into focus as [individuals]. The way to defeat Moosak is quite simple: listen to it."

R. Murry Schafer

ACKNOWLEDGMENTS

The material, published and unpublished, used in the research for this book includes periodicals, a dissertation, interviews, books and other publications. The author is indebted to the following periodicals: Variety, Time, Business Week, Science Digest, Newsweek, Saturday Review, Billboard, New Yorker, Horizon, and Nation's Business. Scholarly and/or professional journals consulted include the Journal of the Acoustical Society of America, Popular Music and Society, Musical Quarterly, Student Musicologists at Minnesota, and Music/The AGO-RCCO Magazine. Charles Black, Jr.'s discussion of the Public Utilities Commission vs. Pollak in the Columbia Law Review is the basis for the commentary in Chapter 6, The Case of the Captive Auditor.

Jerri Husch's dissertation at the University of Massachusets (1984), entitled "Music of the Workplace: A Study of Muzak Culture," provided the foundation for a number of commentaries in this book. To Dr. Husch goes a great measure of gratitude for bringing the implications of Muzak to the scholarly community.

The following books were particularly useful: Charles Diserens, The Influence of Music in Behavior (Princeton: Princeton University Press, 1926); Joseph A. Musselman, The Uses of Music: An Introduction to Music in Contemporary Life (Englewood Cliffs: Prentice Hall, 1974); Donald O'Neill, Scientific Application of Functional Music to Worker Efficiency (New York: Muzak Corporation, 1968); R. Murray Schafer's works in music education provided important background material. They include: The Composer in the Classroom (Toronto: BMI Canada, Ltd., 1965); Creative Music Education: A Handbook for the Modern Music Teacher (New York, Schirmer Books, 1976); and When Words Sing (Scarborough, Ontario: Berandol Music, 1970. The opening quotation in Chapter 6 from Orwell's 1984 is taken from the 1949 edition by Harcourt, Brace (New York).

Promotional material from the Muzak Corporation is used throughout the book and includes the tables and figures used herein. All photos save the portrait of General Squier were used courtesy of UPI/Bettman Archive Photos. General Squier's photo was obtained from the U.S. Army, Fort Gordon, Georgia. My appreciation goes also to the following publishers who have given permission to use their copyrighted material:

Yesterday, Blackwood Music Incorporated, New York.
The Shadow of Your Smile, Columbia Pictures Publications, New York.
Where Do I Begin, Famous Music Corporation, New York.
Someday My Prince Will Come, Bourne Company, New York.
Up, Up, and Away, Jonathan Three Music Company, New York.

Organizations assisting in the completion of this book include the Golden Library, Eastern New Mexico University; the Llano Estacado Center for Advanced Professional Studies and Research at ENMU; and the Department of Art at ENMU.

Individuals involved were Angela De Los Santos, Suzanne Sherman, Donna Powell, Wanda Graham, Laura McGuire, Sherri Johnston, Cindy Roberts, Sharen Hart, and Dr. Everett L. Frost. Without their efforts, the task of producing this book would have been impossible.

Lloyd Wilson and David Noblett designed and typeset the final draft of the text and graphics. To both of them go my deepest appreciation and respect for their pride and professionalism.

Portales, New Mexico
Autumn 1987

INDEX

Studies in The History and Interpretation of Music

1. Hugo Meynell, **The Art of Handel's Operas**
2. Dale A. Jorgenson, **Moritz Hauptmann of Leipzig**
3. Nancy van Deusen, **The Harp and the Soul: Studies in Mediaeval Music**
4. James L. Taggart, **Franz Joseph Haydn's Keyboard Sonatas: An Untapped Gold Mine**
5. William E. Grim, **The Faust Legend in Music and Literature**
6. Richard R. La Croix (ed.), **Augustine on Music: An Interdisciplinary Collection of Essays**
7. Clifford Taylor, **Musical Idea and the Design Aesthetic in Contemporary Music: A Text for Discerning Appraisal of Musical Thought in Western Culture**